Hey, Girlfriend

75 monologues
for girls

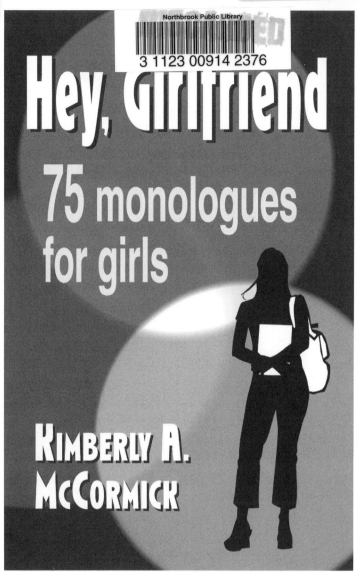

KIMBERLY A. McCORMICK

MERIWETHER PUBLISHING LTD.
Colorado Springs, Colorado

Meriwether Publishing Ltd., Publisher
PO Box 7710
Colorado Springs, CO 80933-7710

www.meriwether.com

Editor: Arthur L. Zapel
Assistant editor: Amy Hammelev
Cover design: Jan Melvin

© Copyright MMIX Meriwether Publishing Ltd.
Printed in the United States of America
First Edition

Library of Congress Cataloging-in-Publication Data

McCormick, Kimberly A. (Kimberly Ann), 1960-
    Hey, girlfriend : 75 monologues for girls / by Kimberly McCormick. -- 1st ed.
    p. cm.
ISBN 978-1-56608-162-7 (alk. paper)
1. Monologues--Juvenile literature. 2. Acting--Juvenile literature. I. Title.
    PN2080.M283 2009
    808.82'45--dc22
                    2009000135

                1   2   3   09   10   11

Dedication

Without my own two daughters, Kaycee and Nicolette, these monologues would never exist. I am eternally grateful for the hours of dialogue my girls are willing to share with me. Through much tears and laughter we understand the need to communicate through all of life's struggles and triumphs. With all of my love, this book is dedicated to my two girls, who graciously allow me to share my opinions, but who are strong enough to form their own.

Table of Contents

Foreword

Teenagers today contend with many more issues than we, their parents, ever had to face. They live in a fast-paced, constantly changing society. They deal with issues that we faced only as adults, or never at all. As teenagers, we never needed to respond to degrading instant message notes. We were not bombarded with sexual television programs and ads. Our teenagers watch these programs and play violent video games. How do we help them sort through the media messages that conflict with our values? How do we help them cope with such a fast-paced life and changing technology? How do we encourage them to counter peer pressure?

Because it's written in teen language, this book of monologues is an answer to these questions. Filled with current topics such as attitudes toward love, education, bullying, and text messaging, it will interest teenagers in high school and middle school. As a middle school teacher, I can attest to the fact that teenagers love role playing. Using these monologues to role play, then discussing the issues will help teenagers put their values into perspective. Kimberly McCormick has included insightful discussion questions at the end of each monologue that parents, teachers, drama coaches, guidance counselors, and other youth leaders can use as a springboard for discussion. Listening carefully to teenagers' responses to these questions helps us understand their viewpoints and enables us to respond in a helpful, non-judgmental way.

I have incorporated scripts from Kimberly McCormick's previous publication, *The Way I See It* for middle school anti-bullying assemblies and teacher workshops with much success. The monologues in *Hey, Girlfriend* are a gift to adults who wish to help teenage girls sort through peer pressure and media messages to become women who reflect our values and morals.

— Mary Ann Wilson
President of Lawrence County Reading Council

Introduction

Hey, Girlfriend is a collection of 75 monologues written specifically with the teenage girl in mind. These monologues may be used for discussion starters, audition pieces, acting exercises, speech competitions, or simply for classroom use. The topics are relevant to today's teenage issues.

These monologues incorporate the four key elements of learning: reading, writing, speaking, and listening. Through these exercises, students have the opportunity to practice in all four modes of learning. Students are asked to present a monologue, which presents an issue relevant to today's teens. Topics range from opinions on dating to our country's involvement in the war. After each monologue, there is a variety of questions related to the monologue's topic. These may be discussed as a class, with the teacher acting as facilitator, or small groups may be formed. The goal of these discussions is that students will have the opportunity to share their view, as well as learn from each other's opinions and knowledge about each topic.

My experience has been that students enjoy incorporating the art of acting into the classroom setting. The acting process allows students the freedom to express themselves through another character. I have witnessed very timid students become outgoing, confident young teens when given the chance to take part in the delivery of a monologue.

It is my wish for you and your students that everyone may become more understanding of each other's opinions and ideas through the use of my monologue collection.

Enjoy!

1. A Selfish Generation

1 Do you realize that our generation has earned the
2 reputation of being selfish? It's true. Ask anyone over the
3 age of forty what their impression is of the majority of youth
4 today, and I'll bet you that the word selfish is mentioned. I
5 can't say that I'm surprised, though. I'm a member of the
6 so-called "selfish generation" and I have to agree. There are
7 a lot of selfish teenagers around.

8 I'm going to include myself in the group as I speak about
9 us, because I'm certainly not perfect. I guess I can see
10 selfishness in some of our everyday attitudes and behaviors.
11 I admit that when I'm asked to do something for my parents
12 that doesn't necessarily fit into my schedule the way I like,
13 I will whine about it and see if I can get out of it. My mom
14 will then remind me that my parents are paying for the car
15 I'm driving, so if she needs me to run an errand for her in
16 that car, I best do it if I'd like to keep driving the car. My
17 selfishness is pretty much squelched at that point.

18 But on a more serious note, I can see that most of us
19 teenagers tend to use our free time to entertain ourselves,
20 rather than helping others. There are always community
21 service projects going on that we could get involved with. A
22 really simple act of giving that doesn't cost us any more
23 than an hour of our time is donating blood. It really is true
24 that you can "donate blood and save a life." I'm thinking
25 about it, but I'm afraid I'll get sick or something.

26 Maybe a better idea for me is the one I read about in the
27 newspaper. There are some schools who accept donations
28 of used homecoming and prom dresses. Girls who are less

1   fortunate can purchase these dresses at the cheapest rates
2   possible. Many of them are given to needy girls. It would be
3   really hard to part with some of my dresses, but if I knew
4   someone who couldn't afford a dress was able to go to a
5   special dance because of my donation, I wouldn't mind
6   giving up a few.
7   You know, I'm tired of hearing about how selfish all of us
8   are. Let's try to change our image today. Think about one
9   way you can begin to help someone in your community,
10 maybe even just someone in your own home. We really need
11 to start showing the older generation that we are going to be
12 able to take over for them one day.

Discussion Questions

Are you able to think of times when you've been exceptionally selfish? Name one thing about yourself you could change to make yourself more giving. Discuss different opportunities in your community in which you could become involved.

2. Will I Ever Fit In?

1   No matter how hard I try, it seems as if I'll never really
2 fit in. I'm not saying that I'm perfect, but all of my friends
3 seem to think that I never do anything wrong. I'm so tired
4 of them acting like I think I'm too good for all of them just
5 because I won't do the things they do.

6   At the last sleepover we had they even started saying
7 how weird it is that my parents are still happily married!
8 How crazy is that? That's pretty sad when people start
9 believing there's something wrong with the couples who
10 stay married for thirty years. I just want to scream at them,
11 "I'm sorry if your parents can't seem to figure out how to
12 keep things together! I'm sorry if they're on husband or wife
13 number three and you're screwed up because of it!"

14   But I don't say anything, because I know my friends are
15 messed up because of the homes they've been raised in.
16 Their parents let them do just about anything they want.
17 They don't care if they're out driving after curfew and my
18 friends can't understand why my parents make me be in by
19 eleven on a junior license. Helloooo! Do they not get it that
20 it's the law? It's not a rule my parents made. It's the law!
21 What kind of parents tell their kids it's OK to break the law?

22   Recently, I made the mistake of doing something I knew
23 I shouldn't do, just so I'd fit in with the group. It was the
24 stupidest choice I ever made so far in my life. It took me
25 three months just to start feeling good about myself again.
26 After that, I vowed I would never allow my friends to make
27 me feel bad about being "good" again.

28   Hey, I'm not perfect and I've never claimed to be. But I

1 don't think we need to do things we know are wrong just
2 because they make us feel good. Some things in life we have
3 to be patient about doing. Most people don't go off driving a
4 car before they're sixteen, or whatever age their state
5 requires. It's just understood you have to wait to be that age
6 in order to drive. So why is it that so many teens are
7 drinking alcohol and having sex? Don't they realize that the
8 day will come when it's OK for us to do those things? But
9 high school is just too soon. I read somewhere that the
10 percentage of high school relationships that last is two
11 percent. Who wants to give up their virginity to those odds?
12   It's easy for people to say to me, "Why don't you just
13 find another group of friends?" Those people obviously
14 haven't been in high school for quite a few years. Changing
15 groups of friends just doesn't happen. My mom says that if
16 I come out of high school with one or two true friends, I'll be
17 really lucky. I'm starting to think she's right.

Discussion Questions

Why do you think it is so difficult for many teens to fit in
during their high school years? Have you ever gone along
with something you didn't feel was right just to maintain
your acceptance in a group? Explain. Is there a time you
spoke up against the group's wishes in order to stay true to
your own beliefs? Explain.

3. Why Don't You Just Kick Me Out?!

1   Most kids have a problem, which is exactly opposite of
2   the problem I'm having. It's time to start looking for
3   colleges, and my parents won't let me consider any school
4   within three hours of home. Why don't they just tell me they
5   want to get rid of me?

6   All of my friends who want to get away from our town
7   are experiencing a different problem. Their parents don't
8   want them to go far from home the first year at school. They
9   say they need a year to adjust to the changes that college
10 brings. Their parents also want to be able to visit them
11 when they're missing them and in case they get sick or an
12 emergency occurs, they're within driving distance of home.

13 Why do my parents feel the opposite of this? Mom and
14 Dad keep telling me that I need to grow up now, and that if
15 I'm too close to home, I'll never really learn to depend on
16 myself. They think I'll just keep running back to them every
17 time there is a problem.

18 I've tried using every valid reason I can think of to
19 convince them to let me go to a school close by. The truth
20 is, I'm not sure I'm ready to be grown up. I know I need to
21 start being more independent of my parents now that I'm
22 eighteen, but do I have to cut the cord the moment I
23 graduate, cold turkey?

24 I think I'd like to go to the university that's just twenty
25 minutes away. It has a good reputation and offers the major
26 I'm interested in. If I get homesick or just need to come
27 home to regroup, I can do that. I'll be glad to help around
28 the house when I stop in, and I promise I won't eat them out

1   of house and home. They always used to say that I did that!
2   I can't stand the thought of leaving for school and being
3   stuck there until Thanksgiving. I won't be able to do it.
4   I've got to think of a way to convince my parents to let
5   me stay close. Any suggestions?

Discussion Questions

What suggestions would you give this speaker? List the pros and cons of going to college close to home and over three hours away. How far away do you plan to go to college? What things are influencing your decision?

4. Who Is Really a True Friend?

1   Why is it we all want to be friends with the mean girl?
2 I've been asking myself this same question for years, as I
3 watch myself grovel and apologize any time she's mad at
4 me.
5   Everyone seems to like her, even though she's cruel and
6 humiliates people. Once I watched her go right up to this
7 poor girl's face and say, "Someone is in desperate need of
8 a fashion emergency." Then she and her entourage laughed
9 their heads off as they strutted away.
10   Why do I want to be friends with a person like this? Is it
11 because I know if I'm not her friend I may become the next
12 recipient of her jokes? Or is it partly because all the guys
13 like her, so I might get to meet some really cool guys?
14   Everything about her is perfect. I've never seen a hair
15 out of place. Her nails are definitely enhancements, always
16 perfectly polished in French manicure style. She probably
17 spends more money in a month on her wardrobe than I've
18 spent during my entire high school career!
19   Last week we were friends, this week it's changed. It's
20 like a roller coaster ride with her. I never know from day to
21 day whether we're on speaking terms or not. Right now
22 she's mad at me because she said something *horrible* about
23 another friend of mine. It was so awful that I won't even tell
24 you what she said. But I will tell you she went borderline
25 psychotic all because of a guy! Well, I told this friend what
26 was said about her, only because it seemed somewhat
27 violent to me, even disturbed. Of course, now *I'm* the one
28 receiving the evil glares because I repeated something told

1   to me.

2   Yet, I find myself writing the mean girl an apology. I
3 offered to go with her to the school counselor if she needed
4 to talk about this situation. She just told me to never speak
5 to her again for the rest of her life. Not only is she mad at
6 me, but her group of friends are treating me as if I'm the
7 walking plague.

8   I know in my own mind this girl is not a true friend. She
9 only decides I'm OK for awhile, when she needs something.
10 Once she gets her favor from me, I'm history, until the time
11 she needs me again.

12   How do I get the courage and strength to not care if I'm
13 a part of this popular group? Whenever I'm outcast like this,
14 I feel worthless ... invisible.

Discussion Questions

Identify the different "groups" of friends that exist in your school. Is there one group you strive to be a part of? How would you handle a friend who only seems to be your friend when they need something? Do you know a person who you try to be friends with, only because to be their enemy would be worse? Is this type of friendship necessary for survival in high school?

5. Who Are My Mom and Dad?

1   Six months ago I found out, completely by accident, that I
2 am adopted. Nothing could have been more surprising to me.
3   I needed to find my birth certificate to arrange some
4 travel plans, so I started rummaging through a drawer of
5 papers kept locked in my dad's office desk. I didn't think
6 he'd care, because all I wanted to find was a birth
7 certificate. When I found it, I was devastated. There were
8 two other people's names listed as my parents, and clipped
9 right to the certificate were my adoption papers. I felt as if
10 my mom and dad had betrayed me. I mean, why wouldn't
11 they let me know after all these years?
12   Mom claims she and Dad planned to let me know once
13 I turned eighteen. I'm not sure why they think eighteen is a
14 magic number. I guess my mom wanted me to be of legal
15 age when I found out, in case I decided I needed to find my
16 birth parents. Maybe that's a reasonable excuse for not
17 telling me sooner, but it's certainly not at all the way I would
18 handle it, if I were a parent.
19   My friends find it hard to believe that I didn't think
20 something was up sooner. Janice asked me, "Didn't you
21 ever ask your mom questions about what it was like when
22 she was pregnant with you, or where you were born?
23 Because my sisters and I have asked my mom lots of
24 questions about way back then."
25   I thought about that for awhile and realized that, since
26 I'm an only child, there were lots of things I didn't ask my
27 mom that children with siblings might have asked. My mom
28 was able to answer the questions I did ask without giving

1   away the fact that I was adopted.
2   Adopted. I think I'm just now coming to terms with the
3   whole idea. At first, I was furious with Mom and Dad. I
4   wouldn't talk to either one of them for three weeks. That's
5   a long time to live in the same house with two people you're
6   not talking to. I spent a lot of time at Janice's. Mom and
7   Dad didn't seem to mind, I think they knew I needed some
8   space.
9   Mom, Dad, and I have spent a lot of time talking about
10 this, though. Things have settled down a lot around home.
11 But I do have this overwhelming desire to go and meet my
12 birth parents. Every man or woman I see on the street who
13 I even vaguely resemble starts me thinking, "Maybe that's
14 my mom or dad." It's crazy! Why would I want to meet
15 people who gave me away, people who didn't want me? But,
16 then I read articles about people who gave their child up for
17 adoption only because they couldn't afford to take care of
18 them, and how they have thought about their baby every day
19 of their life since then. Maybe that's how my birth parents
20 feel.
21   My mom says that when I turn eighteen she'll even help
22 me find my birth parents, if I still want to then. But what I
23 want to know is, "Why should I have to wait? Why can't we
24 look for them now?"

Discussion Questions

At what age do you feel a child should be told if they're adopted? Do you think you would want to find your birth parents if you were adopted? Would you ever consider adoption when you are ready to have children? Why or why not?

6. When Is Joining the War Right?

1   I just learned that my eighteen-year-old cousin signed
2 on with the United States Army. He enlisted! How could he
3 do that without talking to any of us about it? My aunt and
4 uncle were pretty upset at first, but now they've come to
5 accept it.

6   I don't understand how a kid is allowed to sign four
7 years of his life away, especially when our country is at war,
8 without any permission needed from his parents. Is the
9 government saying that we are adults when we reach the
10 ripe old age of eighteen? If that's true, why aren't we allowed
11 to have a drink of beer or a glass of wine until we're twenty-
12 one? Nothing makes sense to me right now.

13   I guess I'm a little angry. No, *a lot* angry with my cousin
14 right now. I mean, we have hung out together on Friday
15 nights since we were in middle school. He fixes me up with
16 his friends, and I do the same for him. I can't believe he
17 didn't ask me my opinion about this before he went and
18 signed up! He probably already knew what my opinion would
19 be, so he didn't want to hear it.

20   I'm scared to death he's going to be killed. He already
21 knows he'll be serving a stint in the war zone. Maybe if I
22 understood the whole point behind the war, I would be more
23 understanding about him being a part of it. I know the
24 troops are helping people gain their freedom, but why don't
25 so many of the people there seem to appreciate our men?
26 What's the purpose of giving your life for a cause if the
27 people you're dying for don't seem to appreciate you?

28   My mom says there are a lot of citizens who are thankful

1 for our troops, but the news enjoys showing the drama of
2 those against our presence more. She said to talk to some
3 of the returning troops and they'll explain to me why what
4 they did was important to democracy.
5   I look at my cousin, and all I see is the little boy I grew
6 up with. I sound old when I reminisce like this, but it's true.
7 We used to swing on the tire out back for hours on a summer
8 morning. Then we'd pack a picnic lunch, tie it up in a
9 handkerchief on a stick, and head for the creek. After
10 skipping rocks on the water for another hour, we'd head
11 home for supper.
12   How did that little boy become the soldier he is now?
13 Why do I still feel so young and helpless, while he looks like
14 the pillar of courage?
15   Lord, I pray for his safety. May this new journey in his
16 life have purpose.

Discussion Questions

Do you feel men and women, age eighteen and older, should have the same rights as twenty-one-year-olds if they're considered old enough to fight in wars? Fortunately, at this time, our county has no draft. How would you feel if the draft system was put back into practice? Would you ever consider a career in the armed forces? Why or why not?

7. Why Does Everyone Care about What We Wear?

1 *(Actor carries a document, which is to be the school dress*
2 *code. Pretend to be reading before speaking, continue to use as a*
3 *prop, referring to the document throughout the monologue.)*
4 I cannot believe this! If you could read what I am
5 reading, you wouldn't believe it either! My school just
6 adopted a new dress code policy. At first I thought, "Well,
7 let me read it. Maybe it won't be so bad." But after I read
8 this, I feel as if the school board is trying to relive their own
9 high school days by making all of us dress the way they had
10 to twenty years ago!
11 Listen to some of this.
12 *No student shall wear a skirt shorter than knee length.*
13 Who in their right mind wears a skirt down to their knees
14 nowadays!
15 *Jeans shall have no more than four pockets.* Have they
16 ever heard of cargo pants? They are so comfortable for
17 sitting in desks seven hours a day! I'm not saying to have
18 them hanging off your butt, I'm just saying there are very
19 few loose fitting jeans that have only four pockets. The four
20 pocket jeans look like you jumped right off your horse from
21 some dude ranch!
22 Oh, but wait, next is *no earrings are to be worn on any*
23 *body part other than the ear. Only one pair shall be worn.*
24 I'm wondering how the school board plans to enforce this.
25 Do they have any idea where some people wear earrings? I
26 won't even go there!
27 Next, *shoes must have closed toes with a back strap.*
28 Can you believe that one? I practically live in my clogs.

1 They're the most comfortable shoes I own. But, clogs with a
2 back strap are definitely uncool. The board claims this rule
3 is for safety reasons. I guess too many people run up and
4 down the stairs and must be tripping on their shoes. I say,
5 "Why not just enforce the 'No running in the halls' rule we
6 already have?"
7   Let's move on. *No collarbones are to show at the*
8 *neckline of your shirt.* So, I guess we are to be buttoned up
9 to the neck! No tank tops, no V-necks, no room to breathe!
10   I don't know. I guess I just thought the school board
11 could have asked a group from student council to meet with
12 them and be involved in the forming of this new policy. There
13 are many more rules here I could read to you, but it would
14 take too long.
15   I'm thinking maybe uniforms would be better than *this*
16 policy!

Discussion Questions

What do you feel is appropriate attire for school? Should
teachers follow the same dress code as the students? What
is your opinion about each of the five rules shared by this
actor?

8. What about Women's Lib?

1   After listening to the most recent argument between my
2 mother and my sister, I'm wondering how I really do feel
3 about women's liberation. When I listen to Mom talk about
4 what things were like when she was young, I agree that
5 fighting for women's rights is essential. But then I listen to
6 my sister talk about the life she chose to step away from in
7 order to be a stay-at-home mom, and it seems as if she is
8 doing the right thing.

9   Candace, my sister, had a fantastic job as a vice
10 president in financing at the bank. When she had my niece,
11 Candace decided she wanted to experience every milestone
12 along the way as my niece grows up. So, she quit her job.

13   Of course, as I could have predicted, my mother just
14 about flipped her lid when she heard. She was close to
15 yelling at my sister, even though it truly is none of her
16 business, since Candace is married and all.

17   Mom's argument sounded something like this,
18 "Candace, how could you give up your career? You have a
19 master's degree and you're choosing to stay at home with
20 your baby? Don't you realize women nowadays can have it
21 all? You could have hired a nanny, and still continued with
22 your career. I will never understand how you could do this!"

23   My sister responded rather calmly given the
24 circumstances, I thought. She simply looked at my mother
25 and said, "Mom, just because your generation of women
26 wanted to get out of the house and have careers, doesn't
27 mean that's what's best for everybody. I've done the career
28 thing for the past ten years. And in those ten years, I have

1 never felt the happiness I've felt with Madison" — her baby
2 — "during the past two months. I'm happy with my decision,
3 so please let's not discuss this any further."
4   "Bravo," I thought. Candace really knows what she
5 wants. It's so strange, though, how my mother had to fight
6 with my father just to get any little job outside of the home.
7 I guess the men back then felt a woman working outside of
8 the home meant that the man of the house wasn't making
9 enough money to support his family. But from the women's
10 point of view, they just wanted to have a life that offered
11 them some choices and a few challenges. My mother said
12 one of her teachers was forced to quit her job as soon as
13 the school board discovered she was pregnant. Can you
14 imagine?
15   Just listening to Candace and my mother's argument
16 made me wonder how I feel about this. Will I want to keep
17 working once I have a child? Candace claims that she and
18 her husband began to experience problems when she tried
19 to keep working. She just couldn't do it all, besides the fact
20 that she wasn't happy with the child care she had. For her,
21 staying at home to raise her baby was her top priority. She's
22 happier. Her husband is happier. It's just the right choice for
23 their family.
24   I also know some women who would like to stay home
25 and raise their children, but they simply can't afford to.
26 Candace is fortunate that way. At least she has the luxury
27 of not working outside the home if that's what she chooses.
28   I have no clue what I'll want in my twenties. I do know
29 one thing, though. It doesn't matter to me what choices
30 other women make about this, I just want to make the right
31 choices for me.

Discussion Questions

Do you ever hear your mother wish for the opposite of what she's now doing? For example, working, if she's a stay-at-home mom, or staying home, if she works? How do you think you will want to handle this when you are older and in this position?

9. True Friendship

1   *(Actor will need five concert tickets in a pocket to pull out*
2   *near the end of the monologue.)*
3   Lately, it's been difficult to know who my true friends
4 are, and who is just being friendly to get something from
5 me. You see, I just won five backstage passes to this
6 awesome concert next month. As soon as the kids in my
7 class heard the news, I suddenly had friends coming out of
8 the woodwork.
9   This whole situation has caused me to stop and reflect
10 upon what true friendship means. There are several kids
11 talking to me now who I would love to be friends with. You
12 know who they are. Members of the popular crowd; kids I
13 never dreamed would want to hang out with me. I keep
14 telling myself that maybe if I take them with me to the
15 concert, they'll see what a nice person I really am, and after
16 the concert, we'll still be friends. But I also remind myself
17 that they are probably just being my friends so that they
18 can go to the concert, and I'll never hear from them again
19 afterward.
20   My group of friends is probably considered the C group.
21 Do you understand what I'm saying? I believe there's this
22 type of hierarchy that goes on in high school. The most
23 popular group is the A group. These are the kids who are
24 beautiful, athletic, get good grades, and never seem to have
25 a problem. The B group is really a pretty nice group of girls
26 who are always striving for the top, but never quite get
27 there. They might be the best group to be in, though,
28 because the A group will talk to most of them. They'll even

1   include them in their group if one of their own is busy.
2   The C group is a little nerdy, and we pretty much stick
3   together. I'm glad I have friends, but sometimes I do wish I
4   could hang out with a group of girls that want to do more
5   than just study or play chess and learn trivia for an
6   upcoming competition. Sometimes I'd rather go shopping or
7   just dance for fun. Even taking a cruise in my mom's car
8   with the music cranked up sounds like more fun than what
9   we do.
10   I think maybe now you understand why I would like to
11 give these tickets to girls I don't really hang out with. Just
12 once I'd like the chance to feel popular and cool. Every time
13 I decide I'm just going to go ahead and invite them to come
14 with me, though, I feel guilty. I have some friends who have
15 stuck by me through some tough times in my life.
16   When my parents were divorced, my C group friends
17 were there for me. When I totally bombed my mid-term in
18 calculus, they were there to tell me things would be all right.
19 Even when my dog was sick and dying, my friends came and
20 spent the night with me in the garage with my dog, offering
21 me the moral support I needed.
22   Wow, when I think of all that my friends have done for
23 me, I feel pretty stupid. How could I have even thought for a
24 millisecond not to take them with me to the concert? I
25 mean, who knows, maybe they feel the same way as I do.
26 Maybe if I asked them to cruise with me in Mom's car,
27 they'd love it! They might even enjoy shopping instead of
28 studying, if one of us would just bring up the idea.
29   Sorry, you A's and B's, the C group has arrived! *(Pulls*
30 *out tickets from pocket and gives them a kiss, or waves them in*
31 *excitement.)* I'm taking my friends to a concert!

Discussion Questions

Do you believe a hierarchy of social groups truly exists in high schools? Is this a snobbish arrangement for students, or just a natural division of girls according to their interests? Do you ever wish to be part of a different circle of friends? Why or why not?

10. Too Much Stress

1   Last week my sociology teacher gave us a question to
2 ponder for awhile. He wanted us to think about just what it
3 is that makes our society dysfunctional. Even families one
4 might consider normal have dysfunctional stuff to deal with.
5 After observing the behaviors of many families, including
6 my own, I've decided the fundamental problem all of us are
7 having is dealing with stress. So, let's ask ourselves, why
8 do we have so much stress?
9   At my house, a lot of stress is caused by our
10 overcrowded schedules. My mom is always flying around
11 trying to figure out how us kids are going to get where we
12 need to be and how we're going to get home. She works full
13 time, so handling a job and being a wife and mother causes
14 a tremendous amount of stress. If one of my younger
15 brothers or sisters gets sick, then there's even more stress,
16 because now Mom and Dad have to figure out who's going
17 to watch the little one.
18   I think we kids in high school have way too much to do.
19 I've heard on television that teenagers get into trouble
20 because they aren't kept busy enough. I'm sure that's true
21 somewhere, but I'd like to know where these idle teenagers
22 are. I don't have one friend who isn't filling every minute of
23 their twenty-four hour day doing something. By the time I
24 spend my day at school, stay afterward for sports, come
25 home and eat dinner, then take a shower, and finally get to
26 my homework, it's time for bed. Before I know it, it's
27 morning and I'm doing the same thing all over again. I don't
28 have time to get into any trouble!

1   Even when I look at the schedule my younger brothers
2 and sisters keep I see stress with a capital *S*. All four of
3 them are involved in some type of dance, sport, or choir. My
4 mom and dad are the typical parents of the twenty-first
5 century; they feel their children have to become involved in
6 things while they're very young, or by the time they're older,
7 they'll be way behind their peers. The sad thing is, they're
8 probably right! I'm only in high school, but even I am able to
9 see that there's an entire generation of kids not being given
10 any time to be kids.
11   Even though Mom and Dad work so hard, there always
12 seems to be some stress over finances. But everything I'm
13 talking about is connected. If we kids weren't in so many
14 activities, there would be more money, right? No money
15 would be spent on lessons, or membership fees, or gas,
16 *especially gas,* to get to all the activities. When there's no
17 money, it's easy to be short-tempered and unkind to each
18 other. Depending on the degree all of this escalates to,
19 divorce happens, or at the very least an unhappy family
20 exists. Thus, we now have dysfunction.
21   Like I said, this is only an example of dysfunction
22 occurring at a somewhat controllable level. Try adding in
23 drugs, alcohol, extramarital affairs, or defiance into the mix.
24 Now that's what I call stress.
25   The answer to all of this seems easy: slow down. Take
26 time to smell the roses as the old saying goes. The funny
27 thing is, as soon as my family tries to actually take a day to
28 relax and do nothing, no one seems happy. Everyone's
29 bored. It's as if we no longer know how to stop and relax.
30 Habits are hard to break.
31   Maybe we need to start trying to form new habits.

Discussion Questions

Do you feel most families are overscheduled with their time? How does your family manage stress? What are some ways your family relaxes together? Share your own ideas on what you believe to be the main cause of dysfunction in a family.

11. Too Much of a Good Thing

1   I am a person who loves holidays. As soon as the first
2 snow falls, I can't wait for Christmas. I've always been that
3 way. Ever since I was a little girl I counted down the days to
4 every holiday I knew about. If it was Easter coming, my
5 mom would help me make a countdown calendar with
6 Easter eggs. If it was Halloween, the calendar had tiny
7 orange pumpkins. Our Christmas countdown calendar had
8 these tiny windows on Santa's workshop that you opened
9 up. Then you'd see a little toy behind the window that the
10 elves were making. We still hang it every year.

11   The thing is, I've noticed that every month new holidays
12 seem to be invented. I know people complain about the
13 commercialism during holidays, but lately I think I have to
14 agree. Honestly, I think the card shops are coming up with
15 new holidays just to boost their business and sell gifts. I'm
16 only in high school, so I don't have the money to buy
17 presents and cards for all of these special days.

18   Did you ever hear of Friendship Day? It's on the first
19 Sunday of August. How about Parents' Day? Fourth Sunday
20 in July. Or maybe you've heard of Grandparents' Day?
21 That's the first Sunday after Labor Day. Actually, I could go
22 on and on. Like I said, I'm a lover of holidays, but I felt really
23 bad last week when it was Sweetest Day, and my boyfriend
24 bought me a gift and I got him *nada. Nothing!* How was I
25 supposed to know when Sweetest Day is? My friends said I
26 should be impressed that he remembered because it's
27 usually the guy who forgets the special days and the girl who
28 remembers. Well, excuse me!

1   When I went to my grandparents recently they were so
2   excited to show me a plant that my cousins sent to them for
3   Grandparents' Day. I felt so bad because I didn't even know
4   the day existed. What was I supposed to say to them? "Uh,
5   sorry, I didn't know there was such a thing as Grandparents'
6   Day." Well, that is what I said, because it was the truth!
7   I don't know. Maybe I'm overreacting, but it just seems
8   like it's all too much of a good thing. Holidays are great, but
9   let's get control of all this nonsense! What will they make up
10   next?

Discussion Questions

Make a list of all the holidays you know. How many do you celebrate? What ideas do you have for a new holiday created by you? What are your feelings about all the holidays that are celebrated? Are they needed or are they a commercial ploy for businesses to make more money? What is your favorite holiday and why is it special to you?

12. The Secret

1   I have been struggling with guilt for the past two
2 months. Every moment of every hour I feel as if I'm going
3 crazy with this secret I'm keeping. If ever I understood what
4 the meaning of a good and bad conscience is, it's now. One
5 second I tell myself this secret needs to be put to rest and
6 forgotten. It's not that big of a deal. No one got physically
7 hurt, so don't worry about it. A moment later, another voice
8 is telling me to speak up, do the right thing. It's just that I
9 have no idea of how vast the consequences might be if I tell
10 the whole truth.

11   You're probably wondering what I'm hiding, right? I
12 guess I can tell you the story. OK, it's like this. About two
13 months ago, I was driving home from practice. Usually I
14 keep my cell phone out on the passenger seat. But that day,
15 I forgot to get it out of my purse, which was on the floor of
16 my car. Just as I approached the intersection close to town,
17 my phone started to ring. It truly crossed my mind to let my
18 voice mail pick up, but then I thought, "What if my mom is
19 calling me and needs me to do something for her while I'm
20 out."

21   So ... you know what I'm going to say next, don't you?
22 You're right.

23   I reached down to the floor for only a second, and when
24 I looked up, I wrecked into a car coming down the street on
25 my left. It happened so quickly. I couldn't believe it! The
26 police arrived before I ever had a chance to talk to anyone.
27 The other driver said I ran the stop sign. Without even
28 thinking, I claimed that he did. Why did I say that? It's been

1 haunting me ever since.

2   Well, when the police took all their measurements and
3 whatever else they do to determine who is at fault, somehow
4 the numbers didn't add up for either of us. There weren't
5 any witnesses, so it became a no-fault case. Both of us had
6 to turn the damage in to our own insurance companies.

7   Do you understand what I mean now? The incident is
8 done — it's over with. No one is hurt, and the cars are fixed.
9 So, why can't I just forget about it?

Discussion Questions

Share a time when you did something wrong and your guilty conscience convinced you to tell the truth. Do you feel this person should fess up to the truth of this accident? Is it ever appropriate to drive and talk on the cell phone at the same time?

13. The Power of Hope

1   Just what is it that makes a young person take their
2   own life? Whenever I hear of tragic news such as this, I have
3   to wonder, "Was there truly nothing at all left in this world
4   for that person to cling to? Or was the timing just bad,
5   where what really mattered in their life just happened to be
6   absent for the moment?" For that brief second when a
7   trigger is pulled or a jump is taken, was a loved one stuck
8   in traffic? Was a cell phone's battery dead? Or maybe a
9   computer virus interrupted that person's cry for help?

10   Regardless of what circumstances lead up to a suicide,
11   a death occurs. A real, blood-pumping, air breathing,
12   human being is forever gone from this world. Why did they
13   not have any hope, not one iota of hope to keep them going?

14   Whose fault is it? Is it anyone's fault when a suicide is
15   committed? Maybe the brain's chemicals are all messed up,
16   so stress in the body just takes over the mind's ability to
17   reason. I don't know. I'm not sure any of us will truly
18   understand what could make a person want to die.

19   What I do know is that sometimes the only thing that
20   keeps me going is the hope that tomorrow will be a better
21   day, even the next hour might be a better sixty minutes than
22   the last sixty. The power of hope is, at times, life-saving.

23   Think of all the occasions in your life when things
24   seemed truly dismal. How was it that you moved past
25   everything that was getting you down? If you really take
26   some time and think about it, I'll bet you started
27   daydreaming and thinking of things you wished would
28   happen. When you focus on positive things you'd like to

1 have in your life, before you know it, you're working and
2 hoping you make those dreams come true.
3   They often say that the people who have survived
4 horrific experiences, like the Holocaust or prison camps
5 during the war, are those who never gave up hope of rescue.
6 Many who quit believing allowed their bodies to shut down
7 and die.
8   Remember, the next time life seems to have you beat, or
9 you're witnessing a friend who's down and out, there is a
10 simple four letter word that can lift you up — it's hope. Hope
11 gives us the inner strength we need to thrive. Hang on to it.

Discussion Questions

From whom do you draw strength and hope when you are going through difficult times? Why do you think some teens are driven to suicide? What can be done to help prevent the feelings of hopelessness they must be experiencing? What might be some warning signs of suicide?

14. The Ideal Teacher

1   Do you think teachers even have a clue as to the impact
2   they can have on students? I started wondering this the day
3   my sister came home from school so upset. Her foreign
4   language teacher collected her homework from her as she
5   walked in the class, looked at it, handed it back to her, and
6   said, "You might as well keep this. It's obvious you didn't
7   even try."

8   Now, I don't know how well my sister did on the paper
9   she turned in, but what I can say is that I witnessed her
10 sitting at the kitchen counter for nearly an hour, with my
11 mom, trying to figure out how to do the homework. Let's
12 face it, not everyone is good at foreign languages. This
13 teacher was way off the mark. My sister may not have done
14 the assignment well, but she definitely tried!

15   I know teaching can be a stressful job. Believe me, I
16 know this because my mom is a teacher. I hear all the
17 horror stories about what they have to put up with. I also
18 know, from a student's perspective, that a teacher can be a
19 negative or positive influence on you the entire year you
20 have them. If teachers would only remember that the time
21 each student spends with them in their classroom just
22 might be the bright spot of the student's entire day, they
23 might try being a little more compassionate. Because the
24 memories of a teacher can either haunt you or motivate you
25 the rest of your life.

26   So, just what is the ideal teacher? I know it's not
27 someone who is always nice. There are times when kids
28 need discipline. And I know that whenever there's someone

1 being totally disruptive in my class, I want the teacher to do
2 something about it. I come to school to learn, and I don't
3 appreciate other kids who are only there to cause trouble.
4 So, an ideal teacher should be someone who can handle the
5 discipline problems in a classroom.
6   I think that being fair is probably one of the most
7 important traits of a teacher. Playing favorites among the
8 students is definitely the wrong thing to do. My favorite
9 teacher was a woman who treated the kids who were
10 obviously poor and perhaps had difficulty in school just the
11 same way she treated the clean-cut, well-off students.
12 Everyone in her classroom felt special. It wasn't that no one
13 ever got in trouble, they did. It's just that she took the time
14 to explain to each student why they were in trouble and
15 what they needed to do to improve. An ideal teacher is a
16 person who loves children, and each child in their class can
17 sense that. I had a friend once who never wanted to go
18 home on Fridays. He said he enjoyed all the work at school
19 a lot more than tiptoeing around his drunk father on the
20 weekends.
21   So, to all of those teachers who are truly burned out, I
22 ask that they question themselves as to why they are still
23 teaching. Is it only for the money? Because if it is, they are
24 negatively affecting a lot of lives, including their own. And to
25 all of you teachers who understand that we students want
26 you to care about us, I say, "Thank you, from the bottom of
27 my heart. Please hang in there. We need you."

Discussion Questions

Describe the ideal teacher. Share examples of times
your own teachers have been there for you. What do you
think an ideal student should be like?

15. The Fake Bake

1   OK, I agree that a person with a tan looks great. In fact,
2   when I don't have a little sun, I feel like I look sickly. But,
3   have you noticed how many girls are taking the fake bake a
4   little too far? I see these salons that offer unlimited tanning
5   packages, and I wonder how many girls salon-hop from one
6   to the other all in one day? Their skin is going to look like
7   shriveled prunes by the time they're twenty-five!

8   I do get really confused when I try to research and learn
9   about the risks of tanning. I know any exposure to UV rays
10 can be harmful, but it's also healthy to be out in the
11 sunshine. Being in the sun causes our bodies to generate
12 Vitamin D, which we need to have strong bones. Where I
13 live, we have very few sunny days, so I go in a tanning bed
14 once a week. Am I causing harm to myself, or helping
15 myself?

16 Another reason I like to tan is because it is so dreary
17 around here. I think I might have that syndrome I've heard
18 about where people's moods are dramatically affected by
19 the lack of light. When I'm feeling depressed, it just feels so
20 good to get into the warm tanning bed. That fifteen minutes
21 of warmth and light can completely lift my dark mood.

22 *Then* I pick up a magazine that's showing all these
23 young girls in their twenties who have skin cancer. It says
24 that ninety percent of skin cancer is caused by sun
25 exposure. I get really scared when I hear that. I start
26 checking every mole on my body and worrying if I get an
27 extra freckle! I'm not sure what's safe and what's not.

28 My mom has always told me that if I'm going to swim

1   and am in the sun it's best to have a base tan so I don't get
2   burned. I do seem to have skin that tans well, and I always
3   use sunscreen. So, I think I'm doing everything I can do to
4   be a safe tanner.
5   I don't know if I'm right or not, but it seems that famous
6   old saying, "Do everything in moderation," might apply here.
7   Let's all try not to become sun addicts, but just healthy
8   tanners. Is that even possible?

Discussion Questions

Is it ever OK to tan in the sun? What are the dangers? How can you prevent getting skin cancer? Are you aware of your skin type and how much sun is safe for you to get? What other options to tanning are there?

16. The Decline of Morality

1   Lately, I've been taking a long look at some of my
2 favorite TV shows. I love to watch the teen soap opera type
3 shows. To me, they are pretty realistic. A lot of the teen
4 storylines seem true to the lives of modern day teens. The
5 girls and guys deal with drugs and alcohol, sex, teen
6 pregnancy, truancy, failing grades, and just plain meanness
7 toward others. There's always drama about who's dating
8 who and what girl is getting in the middle of someone's
9 relationship. I see so many of these same problems in my
10 own school that I could probably contribute a few storylines
11 for future shows myself!

12   The scary part is that a lot of my friends seem to base
13 their decisions on the message TV is sending them.
14 Because the majority of teen soaps show the couples
15 having sex, most of my friends think it's OK. They'll make
16 comments like "It's not a big deal. Haven't you kissed a
17 bunch of guys? Well, having sex is just going a little further
18 than that. So what if you're with more than one guy in a
19 lifetime. Everyone is!" Sometimes I catch myself wondering
20 if they're right. It does seem as if everyone is doing it. I
21 guess I just always thought you were supposed to be
22 married or in love, at the very least.

23   The media also makes drinking look like so much fun,
24 especially on the reality shows. Everyone says how much
25 more relaxed they are after they've put down a few. Because
26 of that, now my friends have decided we should get some
27 alcohol before the next school dance. I don't want to be a
28 priss or a tattletale, but I'm really not into any of the things

1 my friends are wanting to do.

2   I don't usually think of myself as a prude, but lately I've
3 been thinking that I must be. I try to be respectful to my
4 parents and other adults. I don't drink, smoke, or use weed.
5 I go to church at least twice a month and always make
6 curfew. I'd be stupid not to because I'd lose my right to the
7 car on the weekends. I almost had sex once, but that was
8 just a stupid situation.

9   Every time I'm faced with a difficult decision about my
10 belief system, I hear this tiny voice inside my head telling
11 me "Stop! Don't do it!" It's really weird, but that tiny voice
12 sounds just like my mom's! It's like I can't get away from
13 her even when she's not around. I guess all the talks we had
14 must have really sunk in. She seems to keep me in line even
15 when she's not with me.

16   My question is, "Whose voice do my friends hear inside
17 their heads when they're experimenting in risky stuff?" Are
18 they listening to the morals TV is teaching us? Do they just
19 ignore what their parents taught them and do whatever feels
20 good? I'm sure they probably don't feel good after. Or maybe
21 they really don't care. It's just hard for me to believe that
22 their morals have changed so much since junior high.

23   I guess the only advice I can offer you, and me, is to stay
24 true to the person you were as a child. Don't lose that
25 innocence. Childhood was a time when we believed our
26 parents could do no wrong. I'm starting to think that maybe
27 I was pretty lucky to get the parents I have. All those beliefs
28 they pounded into my head when I was younger are starting
29 to make a lot of sense to me now.

30   Ooooh, that's scary. I never thought that I'd hear myself
31 say that!

Discussion Questions

Do you find yourself being influenced by TV shows and what the teens on those shows are doing? Explain. Are there any moral beliefs your parents have passed on to you that you find yourself questioning? How do you decide which morals will become a strong part of your own belief system?

17. Texting Terror

1 There are no words to describe the horrible feelings I
2 have right now. I have dealt with guilt before, but never, ever
3 this way. I took another person's life. Yeah, that's right. I
4 didn't try to, but it was my fault a man died. It was a terrible
5 accident. I relive it every waking moment, and even though
6 it's been months since it happened, the scene plays through
7 my mind as if it was just yesterday.

8   I left for school like any other morning. It seemed like it
9 was going to be a great day. The weather was clear and not
10 too warm. The sun was shining. I had cheerleading practice
11 after school, and I was already psyched about that. We had
12 a competition coming up that weekend and we planned to
13 win.

14   Just as I turned onto the road leading to my school, my
15 cell phone went off. My parents had told me and told me
16 never to use my cell phone while driving. And the truth is, I
17 never did. I don't know what made me reach for my phone
18 this time. What was it that made me feel the need to break
19 my parents' rule? To break *my* rule? I knew not to talk or
20 text on the phone while driving. God, how I wish I could
21 relive that single moment when I reached for my phone.

22   I could tell by the ring it was a text message. I think in
23 my own mind I felt that I could easily look down and read
24 the message without losing control of my car. And I did do
25 that part OK. But, like an absolute idiot, I tried answering
26 the text back while driving.

27   Oh, I know, there are lots of people who say they have
28 no problem whatsoever texting and driving. But I can tell

1　you this: It never crossed my mind that I would have a
2　problem either. As soon as I started to type my response, I
3　heard a bang on my windshield. Glancing up, I let out such
4　a bloodcurdling scream. I slammed on the brakes, but it was
5　too late. I had hit a man who was riding his bike alongside
6　of the road.
7　　　That's when things begin to get a little blurry. I try to
8　remember the rest, but the only thing I remember from that
9　point on is the fact that I am responsible for another human
10　being's death. I could be sitting in jail right now on
11　involuntary manslaughter charges. The only reason I'm free
12　to talk to you now, and not sitting in a cell somewhere, is
13　because the man's family offered me forgiveness. They told
14　me that if I would send the message out to other teens
15　about my experience, maybe I could help save another
16　person's life. So, I'm trying to speak to as many groups of
17　teens as I can arrange.
18　　　That man's family is awesome. I can only imagine what
19　a wonderful man he must have been. While they say they
20　have forgiven me, I don't know if I can ever forgive myself.
21　Do you know what the most shameful part of all of this is?
22　The text I received said "Tornado cheerleaders r #1." I was
23　texting back, "We r the best!" And for that, a man died.

Discussion Questions

How do you feel about cell phone usage while driving?
Has this practice ever caused you or anyone else you know
to be in an accident? Tell what you should do if you receive
a call or text while you're driving.

18. STD = You're Not Immune!

1   Wow — I've just been hit with some major news,
2 something I haven't quite fully processed yet. I'm trying to
3 remain calm, but I'm on the edge here. Some girl just
4 approached me, introduced herself as my boyfriend's ex-
5 girl, and told me that she has an STD ... *that he gave her!*
6 I'm sure my mouth is still hanging wide open from the
7 shock.

8   Right now, I'm trying to convince myself that this girl is
9 seeking revenge on my guy because he dumped her. But
10 truthfully, she seemed pretty sincere. In fact, she even had
11 tears in her eyes when she told me about this. Her story is
12 that she never slept with a guy until Brian. She claims Brian
13 has HPV and that he won't admit it. When she told him that
14 she has HPV, he tried accusing her of sleeping around.

15   I have been told by other people that Brian has been
16 around a little. Well, maybe even a lot. He doesn't deny that
17 he's slept with other girls. I guess it bothered me some, but
18 nowadays, there don't seem to be many guys who haven't
19 already been with a girl in that way. Brian said he loves me,
20 and he was ready to commit to me. Otherwise, I never
21 would have dated him, just because of the reputation he
22 has. But now, I'm not sure if it's worth it.

23   His ex said the doctor even suspects her case has
24 developed into a cervical cancer, and she's scheduled for
25 surgery next week. I asked her why she felt she needed to
26 tell me all this personal stuff when I don't even know her.
27 That's when she started to cry and said that she knew Brian
28 would never tell me what he knows is true about himself.

1   She thought she would feel guilty the rest of her life if she
2   didn't warn me about this.
3   I guess guys can have HPV and not even know it. Unless
4   they have an outbreak of warts, they can carry the virus and
5   pass it on without ever being aware. Brian's ex said this
6   must be Brian's situation, because she can't seem to get
7   through to him that he is a carrier. She also promised me
8   over and over again that she has never slept with another
9   guy besides Brian.
10   Brian and I have really just started up this relationship
11 thing. As disappointed as I am with what this girl told me, I
12 guess I'm truly thankful she came forward. I'm thanking God
13 right now that I haven't slept with Brian. Maybe it's unfair to
14 him, but I'm really wrestling with whether or not I want to
15 pursue this relationship any further. I like him a lot, but I
16 don't know if I want to deal with this the rest of my life. My
17 confusion may lie in the fact that I don't know much about
18 HPV. Can anyone help me out here?

Discussion Questions

What is HPV? Should you be worried about contracting this virus? How can this be prevented? How much of your sexual history do you feel you should be obligated to share with a new partner? Do you think your relationship would be affected by the news that your boyfriend has an STD?

19. Stay Home, Mom and Dad!

1   I'm going to share something with you that I know is
2 wrong, but I just can't help feeling the way I do. I am
3 embarrassed of my mom and dad. I know it's not right to
4 feel that way, but whenever they come to anything at
5 school, I look around and see other people whispering about
6 them. Some of the kids actually laugh at them. It makes me
7 feel so bad, but I know that my life would be much easier if
8 they just stayed at home!

9   Kids are cruel. They always have been and probably
10 always will be. Both my mom and dad are really overweight.
11 They weren't always that way. Whenever I look at old photos
12 of them from their high school days it's hard to believe they
13 are the same people. I don't understand how they could
14 have let themselves get this way. I mean, I'm talking a good
15 seventy-five to a hundred pounds overweight. Not only am I
16 embarrassed by the way they look, but I'm worried about
17 them for health reasons.

18   It seems like the only thing they enjoy doing together is
19 eating! One time I tried talking to them about it, but my
20 mom started to cry, so my dad got really defensive about it.
21 He told me that they love each other just the way they are
22 and that I didn't need to worry about anyone's weight in the
23 family but my own. I told him that I'm worried about them
24 because they both have high blood pressure. His answer to
25 that was that they take pills to control it and so I didn't
26 need to worry about that either.

27   What am I supposed to do? I love my parents, but I'm
28 tired of being the girl who has the fat parents. I'm really not

1   all about appearances, but it hurts to know the other kids
2   make sick jokes about them. I've come really close to
3   asking my parents to stay home from my basketball games.
4   I know it would hurt them, but do they understand how it
5   hurts me to hear what's being said about them behind their
6   backs? Do they not realize how people stare at them?
7   Someone give me some advice here, because I don't know
8   what to do.

Discussion Questions

Are you ever embarrassed by your parents' appearances? What are some things your parents do that embarrass you in front of your friends? Do you believe your embarrassment is justified or are they things that teens need to accept as simply being differences between the generations? What advice would you give this girl in order to help her parents reach a healthy weight? Should she ask her parents to stay at home from her games so that her classmates will stop making fun of them?

20. Stale Relationships

1   Can anyone tell me what happens to great relationships
2   once they've lasted a few years? I've been dating the same
3   guy since junior high, and now that it's time to go to
4   college, both of us are thinking that maybe we should break
5   up. It's not that I want to — I love my boyfriend. But I feel
6   as if we see each other out of habit sometimes. I just don't
7   feel that excitement I used to feel when we first started
8   dating. I don't think he does either, but we still get along
9   great. This just doesn't make any sense to me.
10   It's like there's no longer any anticipation about getting
11   together, it's just understood. My mom says that what
12   we're going through is normal, that all relationships have
13   times that are a little boring, and that it's up to both of us
14   to create some fun. It just seems like that's a lot of work.
15   Why should you have to create fun for both of you, shouldn't
16   it just happen?
17   I have heard my mom and dad say that the reason their
18   marriage is still together is because both of them work at it.
19   Relationships are all about keeping promises that you've
20   made to each other. Greg and I did promise each other to
21   always be there for one another. But lately, I've found myself
22   being attracted to other guys. Mom says you never stop
23   finding people attractive just because you're in love with
24   one guy. You just know that you are to honor your promise
25   and stay true to each other.
26   She doesn't really care if Greg and I break up. She just
27   said I need to think really hard about it first and talk to Greg
28   about it. I guess I can't imagine being with another guy,

1 Greg is so dependable and always there for me. But going
2 off to college two hours away almost seems like the perfect
3 time to try going it alone. I'm really confused about things
4 right now.
5   It's like I want to see what it's like to be single as a
6 college student. I haven't been without a boyfriend since the
7 eighth grade. But I want to keep Greg on the "back burner"
8 in case I don't like being single. I know that's not right, but
9 I don't want to give him up unless I'm sure I'll be OK without
10 him. And I just don't feel that certain about it yet. Have any
11 of you ever gone through this? Please, give me some advice.

Discussion Questions

If you've been in a relationship for a while, please share the ups and downs of what most relationships experience. Do you believe it takes hard work to keep a relationship together? Explain. Is it reasonable for one to think you can keep a relationship going if the two people are living over two hours away from each other?

21. Sisters!

1   When I was an only child I used to beg my parents for a
2 baby brother or sister. I came up with every reason under
3 the sun as to why we needed another child in the house. My
4 parents would just laugh and tell me that I should enjoy
5 being an only child, because I was able to have more and do
6 more, since they only had one child to pay for. They were
7 never able to convince me, though.

8   When I was eight I devised a plan. I came up with a list
9 of reasons we should have a baby around. I even made up
10 a presentation and shared it with my parents. I was quite
11 the young salesperson. My reasons were: I was definitely
12 lonely and needed a playmate and I would need a sister or
13 brother once my parents were old. Of course, I promised I
14 would help my parents take care of the baby.

15   Looking back, I think I was mostly just jealous of my
16 friends who had brothers and sisters. I wanted to be like
17 everyone else. There was just something not quite right
18 about being an only child.

19   You can only imagine how happy I was when Mom and
20 Dad told me my wish was coming true. Sure enough, after
21 months of waiting, my little sister arrived. Here's the
22 problem: The fun lasted about two weeks! She's been
23 nothing but a pain in the neck ever since. What in the world
24 was I thinking? It's been ten years of crying and whining
25 ever since!

26   I can't begin to tell you how having another child in the
27 family has disrupted my life! The first big change was I had
28 to give up playing softball. My mom said that she couldn't

1 handle running me to more than one practice, so I had to
2 choose between softball and cheerleading. I chose the
3 cheering but I still miss playing ball.
4   Then, I had to give up my bedroom. Mom and Dad said
5 my old bedroom was warmer and better suited for a baby,
6 so I had to move into the bigger, colder bedroom. Ten years
7 later, I'm still in the cold bedroom.
8   I remember when Mom used to come home from
9 shopping trips with little surprises she found for me. Now
10 she says that extra money has to go toward the new
11 addition to the family. I say, "Wait a minute! Who asked for
12 this tiny person to come into our household, anyway?"
13   Don't say to me, "You did." I know I did, but I had no
14 idea how much I would have to give up just to have a baby
15 sister. Why didn't someone warn me? Why didn't someone
16 tell me that things would never be the same in my life again
17 once the baby arrived?
18   When I complain, some of my friends ask me, "Do you
19 even love your little sister?" That makes me feel really bad
20 because I know I do. It's just that life was a lot more fun
21 before she came around, and I don't think it will ever be that
22 much fun again.

Discussion Questions

Can you relate to any of the comments this person is saying? What do you think the pros and cons of being an only child are? What about the pros and cons of having sisters and brothers in your family? Do you think it matters how many years are between brothers and sisters? If you could plan the ideal family size, how many would that be? What advice would you share with this person to help her be happier in her situation?

22. Single and Loving It

1   Two months ago I could not have stood here before you
2   and talked about my broken relationship with my ex-
3   boyfriend. I was a mess. It was hard for me to even get out
4   of bed in the morning. You see, we dated for three years. I
5   never thought he would break up with me, let alone cheat
6   on me, then lie to me about it. That just wasn't the guy who
7   I fell in love with. He would never have done something like
8   that. But I guess I'm learning that even the best people
9   change.
10   Eric and I just seemed to click, ever since junior high.
11 He was my best friend. Oh, I still had my girlfriends, but if
12 I had a choice, I'd be with Eric rather than them. I trusted
13 him more than my girlfriends. I love my friends, but girls
14 just seem to have more trouble keeping secrets than guys.
15 Eric always seemed to know the right things to say to make
16 me feel better.
17   This is our senior year, and I thought it would be our
18 best yet. Instead, it was our last year together. I'd like to
19 pretend that there's still a chance for us to get back
20 together, but that's all it would be — pretending. I did that
21 for awhile. It gets old. I laid around thinking about all the
22 wonderful times we spent together. I want to keep all of my
23 memories, because those three years are really special to
24 me. But I have to accept that Eric has moved on.
25   My friends allowed me to have a pity party for myself for
26 a few weeks, then they laid into me. As harsh as it seemed
27 at the time, it's exactly what I needed. My friends knew that
28 I had grieved Eric long enough; it was time to get mad. I had

1 to realize that I deserved better. True love is not about
2 cheating and lying to someone. When you love someone, you
3 work out your problems. If you're questioning whether or not
4 to continue your relationship, you talk about it together. You
5 don't go off with someone new before you've finished the
6 relationship you're in.
7   I know people make mistakes, and then need
8 forgiveness, but he's not asking for forgiveness. He's moved
9 on and left me behind. I think he enjoyed knowing that I was
10 crying and wanting him back. Well, guess what, Bud! I'm
11 over you. The tears are done and I'm ready to live my life!
12 No more planning around you and your agenda. I'm on my
13 own agenda now and I've got plans for me. Look out, world!
14 I'm single and I'm lovin' it!

Discussion Questions

What are some important characteristics of a healthy relationship? Do you think high school students should be involved in serious relationships or are they too young? If you want to break off a relationship you are in, how can you do this and cause the least amount of hurt to the other person? Do you think it's normal to be attracted to other people when you are in love with someone?

23. When to Tell Secrets

1   I have been keeping this secret my friend shared with
2 me for a long time. At first, her problem seemed minor, I
3 wasn't really concerned. But now, I'm very concerned, and I
4 know it's time I need to tell someone about her secret. I'm
5 just afraid I'll lose her friendship if I do.

6   My friend has been losing all kinds of weight. She never
7 was overly heavy, maybe five to ten pounds overweight I'd
8 guess. But once she started on this diet, nothing is stopping
9 her. Every time someone pays her a compliment for looking
10 so good, it seems to make her want to lose even more. I
11 keep telling her she needs to stop dieting, because she
12 looks great the way she is. She's actually too thin right now,
13 if you ask me.

14   Honestly, I think she's anorexic. You know, the disorder
15 where you starve yourself. I looked up all the symptoms on
16 the Internet when I suspected this. My friend does really
17 weird things. Like, she'll go to the library during study hall
18 and look through food magazines the entire period. She'll
19 bake cookies, then bring them to school and pass them off
20 on everyone else, never eating one herself. She is constantly
21 talking about her weight and how heavy she is. It's like she
22 wants all of us to keep telling her, "No, you're not fat! You're
23 so skinny." She seems to thrive on hearing those words.

24   Finally, she confessed to me yesterday that she is
25 taking laxatives. When I questioned her, she said she was
26 having trouble going to the bathroom and that she needed
27 them. She went on to say, very defensively, I might add,
28 that her mother knew she was taking them, so if I thought

1 I needed to tell on her, go right ahead, because it wouldn't
2 matter anyway. Then she added, "But this is a secret
3 between you and me, right?"
4   I don't know. It seems like she's wasting away to
5 nothing. I have to wonder if her parents don't notice this.
6 Her clothes are oversized, so maybe they don't. I'm really
7 not sure who to tell. I don't want to say anything because I
8 don't want to lose my friend. I never see her eat more than
9 a bit of apple every day at lunch. I think she's starving
10 herself to death.
11   I know if I tell someone, she's going to be furious with
12 me. *(Pause, thinking)* I guess the loss of a friendship is better
13 than the death of a friend. Maybe I'll go talk to her mom
14 after school.

Discussion Questions

Share with your group what you know about eating disorders. Have you ever known someone experiencing an eating disorder? What are the signs and symptoms? Discuss healthy weight loss programs as well as maintenance plans.

24. Put-Downs

1   All my life I've tried to be kind to others, not just to the
2 cool kids in my class but also the kids classified as geeks
3 and dorks. I guess that's something both my grandma and
4 mom taught me. If someone is always the last one to be
5 picked for a team in gym class, I'd always pick them close
6 to first, after I picked my best friends, of course. Even if
7 someone was sitting by themselves in the lunch room, I'd
8 go over and ask them to join my friends and me.

9   But now I'm realizing that just being nice maybe isn't
10 going far enough. You see, for the first time, I am the
11 receiver of a lot of rudeness and cruel comments. It just
12 started this year. I put on a few pounds over summer, which
13 I'm trying to lose, but am having trouble doing. I was
14 walking down the hall last week when a group of the football
15 players started yelling, "Hey, B.B., how's it going?"

16   I just kind of waved and thought, "That's weird. Why are
17 they calling me B.B.?" Over the past week it has continued
18 until finally I came right out and asked, "What the heck are
19 you guys calling me B.B. for? My name is Bonita!"

20   One guy yelled back, "Don't you know? It's 'cause you
21 got that really Big Butt thing goin' on this year. That's OK,
22 darlin'. We like it!" Then the hooting and laughing went on
23 as I turned around and walked away. I wanted to put my
24 books behind my butt so they couldn't see it and make any
25 more fun of me.

26   I'm not sure I've ever felt so humiliated in my life, which
27 is why I'm thinking just being nice to people who get picked
28 on is not enough. Someone needs to stand up to these

1 bullies when they act this way. And now that I've had time
2 to think about it, you can bet those guys are going to receive
3 an earfull from me the next time they call me B.B.
4   Students who witness other students being harassed
5 need to not only befriend these people, but get a group of
6 friends together who have the courage to stand up to the
7 bullies. Actually, bullies probably need help themselves.
8 Most bullies only pick on other people because they don't
9 feel good about who they are. Being a bully identifies them
10 as something, even if it's the class bully.
11   I've also made a pact with my friends: Every day we give
12 each other compliments to build ourselves up. Usually we
13 gather and complain about this and that, putting ourselves
14 down. I realize now that our job is to lift each other up.
15 Think how good you'd feel if every day you came to school
16 you knew that your friends were going to be there, making
17 you feel good about yourself.
18   Yeah, we've got a plan here. Life is too short to be
19 worrying about what others think. We have to create our own
20 positive surroundings. Even if the guys keep calling me B.B.,
21 I know my friends are going to be calling me Bonita, which,
22 by the way, means pretty!

Discussion Questions

Have you ever witnessed others putting someone down?
Share ways that you can help that person. Have you ever
been the victim of harassment? Tell ways you can maintain
a positive self-image, despite put-downs.

25. Promises between Friends

1   I just visited a friend. Well, at least this person I sat next
2 to had the same name as my friend. They say she's the
3 same person I knew. I sat next to Katy for one hour, trying
4 to find a glimmer of who she used to be inside the shell of
5 a body she now has.

6   You see, my friend was in a car accident a year ago. She
7 made the mistake of getting into a car with someone who
8 had been drinking. It was a rainy night. The roads were wet,
9 dangerous to drive on, even if you're sober.

10   It was my friend's first date with a guy she'd been crazy
11 about our entire sophomore year. He finally asked her out,
12 and she was so excited to be invited to a senior party. I
13 guess some of the seniors had beer and wine. Katy didn't
14 drink. We always talked about underage drinking and how
15 stupid we thought it was. Katy and I were athletes and we
16 played on all the sports teams together since we were in
17 third grade. We agreed we'd never do drugs or drink. Why
18 put something so harmful into our bodies?

19   That's why I was so shocked when I heard Katy was in
20 a drunk-driving accident. My first thought was, "How could
21 that be when she promised me, we promised each other,
22 we'd never drink?" But then all the facts came out. Katy
23 didn't have any alcohol in her. I should have known better
24 than to ever doubt her.

25   It was Matt, the kid she liked so much. Other kids at the
26 party said he had a few drinks. He wasn't noticeably drunk,
27 but it was enough to cloud his judgment, to make his
28 reactions slow. It was enough that he lost control of his car

1   and slammed into a telephone pole. Katy had her seatbelt
2   on and was still thrown through the windshield. Her skull
3   was fractured, she had broken ribs, a broken arm, and over
4   a hundred stitches in her face to put it back together.
5   Katy can't talk or walk. This beautiful, vibrant friend I
6   had is now just a body sitting in a chair or lying in a bed. I
7   try to see her at least once every few weeks. Sometimes I
8   ask myself why, because I'm not sure if she even knows I'm
9   there. But as long as she's alive, there's hope. I like to think
10 she knows I'm still there for her, praying she'll come back to
11 us.
12   If there's one thing I would change about the promise
13 Katy and I made to each other, it would be to never get in a
14 car with someone who has been using drugs or alcohol. You
15 know what, why don't you make that promise with your best
16 friend right now?

Discussion Questions

What are the possible consequences of drinking and driving, or simply riding in the car with someone who's been drinking? Define the term "involuntary manslaughter" and its consequences. Make a pact with your friends right now to never drink and drive, or even ride in a car with someone who's been drinking.

26. Opportunity Knocks

1   I am totally psyched! We just came from an assembly
2 where a college recruiter talked to us about all the
3 opportunities we have waiting for us once we get to college.
4 I don't think I even realized what all is out there for me.
5 From the time I was little, I thought I would either be a
6 teacher or a nurse. But after listening to this lady, I realize
7 there are so many fields to choose from that I don't have a
8 clue what I want to study.

9   One thing I never thought of studying until today is
10 meteorology, you know, the study of the weather. I've
11 always been fascinated by the weather; in fact, even a little
12 frightened. But maybe if I study and learn more about it, I'll
13 have less fear, and maybe even become a weather woman
14 on TV. Now that I think about it, I would absolutely love to
15 do it, because not only am I interested in the weather, but
16 I've always wanted to learn about broadcasting and
17 communications.

18   Or maybe I'll be an architect. I've always been good at
19 math and drawing, which are two skills I think architects
20 need. I could design huge buildings for large cities, where
21 there are rooftop gardens and enclosed walkways joining
22 the buildings. I'd have large aviary rooms where plant life is
23 abundant, and birds can fly freely. Just imagine all the
24 things I could do!

25   Of course, there's nothing wrong with following my
26 original plan. We still need teachers and nurses, and both
27 are noble professions. But maybe, just maybe, I'd rather be
28 the superintendent of schools or a surgeon instead of a

1 nurse. Those are the kinds of choices I'm allowed to make!
2   The woman said that it takes two years of study just to
3 finish your required classes. During those two years, I can
4 go to school with an undeclared major. That way, I can try
5 out a lot of different classes and try to figure out what I
6 really want to pursue for my degree. The hardest thing is
7 going to be deciding on one thing. There are so many
8 opportunities out there for us girls nowadays that it's going
9 to be hard to pick!
10   I was also impressed that the recruiter didn't try to tell
11 everyone that college is the only way to go. She made it
12 quite clear that not all of us should go to school. Some
13 people are better suited to vocational trade schools.
14   The point that the recruiter wanted to make, though,
15 was that everyone needs to have some type of skill to offer
16 the world. Whether it is college or a trade school, try to
17 make the most of your potential talents as much as
18 possible. Don't settle for something less than you are.
19   I don't know about you, but I can't wait to graduate high
20 school and move on to the next chapter of my life. Look out
21 world, here I come!

Discussion Questions

List all of your passions and interests. Write down as many jobs related to these interests that you can think of. Think about a job related to these which you could pursue. If you could have your dream job, what would it be? What steps do you need to take to reach this goal?

27. Nowhere to Turn

1   I have nowhere to turn. Everything in my life is a mess.
2 My mom is hung-over any time she happens to be home, my
3 dad took off about six months ago, and my little brother is
4 already dealing drugs. I've been working at McDonald's just
5 to have some spending money and save the rest.
6   Tonight my mom just found out I've been working. She
7 demanded that I give her any money I had. There's no way
8 I was going to give her my money. I knew she'd go spend it
9 on booze, maybe even drugs. So, I told her I didn't have any.
10 She started slapping me and screaming, "Liar, liar!" in my
11 face. I finally pulled out a ten dollar bill and gave it to her.
12 She didn't believe that was all I had, but it seemed to pacify
13 her, so I could get out the door for work.
14   When I got home, I found my room in shambles. My
15 mom tore my room apart looking for more money. Sure
16 enough, she found it. I was saving a small bit to put toward
17 college. I had nearly five hundred dollars saved. It's all gone
18 now.
19   I can't explain to you how I'm feeling right now. A part
20 of me wants to run away, as far away from her as possible.
21 Yet, unbelievably, there's a part of me that just wants to
22 grab my mother in a big hug and tell her I still love her, and
23 that she needs to get some serious help before she destroys
24 herself and everyone she loves. Then, I stop, and I ask
25 myself, "Does she even love me anymore? Or have her
26 addictions replaced any love she may have had for me?"
27   I don't know where, or who, to turn to next.
28

Discussion Questions

If this girl was your friend, what advice would you give her? What resources are available for teens in trouble? (The teacher should be aware of local counseling services available for teenagers and share these with the group once the group members have expressed their own ideas.)

28. No One Likes a Bully!

1   Ever since I was a little kid I can remember the other
2   students in my classes who were bullies. I've always
3   wondered what makes a person want to be that way toward
4   others. I mean, our world is made up of people with so many
5   differences. Life would be boring if everyone was exactly the
6   same and everyone had the same beliefs and opinions. But
7   each day, we see people acting out against one another
8   because people look different or have different opinions.
9   We pride ourselves for living in the "land of the free."
10 There are few limits to those freedoms when you think
11 about it. We can dress how we wish, pretty much say
12 whatever we want to, worship our own God, and live a
13 meaningful life with little fear.
14   For many, when they try to enjoy these freedoms, others
15 ridicule and bully them. Heaven help the student who is too
16 thin, or too fat, or too short, or too tall. Half of the things
17 kids pick on each other about are things that nature has
18 given us, and we can't really do a thing about them.
19   When people don't feel good about themselves on the
20 inside, they can turn into mean, ugly creatures. No one
21 comes into this world a bully. Bullies are created. We all can
22 make the choice to start being kind to everyone, regardless
23 of how different they are from us. Once a person feels
24 respected by others they start to give respect.
25   I'm not saying that a person who is way different than
26 you are has to become your best friend, but what would be
27 wrong with saying, "Hey, what's up?" when you see them in
28 the hallway? Just acknowledge they exist. Maybe bullies act

1 out because at one time, no one even noticed them. Bullying
2 isn't a great way to get noticed, but to some kids it's better
3 than not being noticed at all.
4   I know that I don't have the answer to bullying, but I do
5 know that it will take all of us to stop it from happening.
6 When you see it going on, have some courage. Help the poor
7 kid out who's being picked on. Speak up. It starts with one
8 voice standing up for yourself or someone else.
9   Honestly, no one likes bullies, including the bullies
10 themselves.

Discussion Questions

If you are comfortable in doing so, share a time when you have been bullied by someone. Have you ever witnessed bullying? Explain. What did you do, or could you have done, to help the person being bullied? In your group, share ways you believe students can help to put a stop to bullying.

29. Negative People

1   Have you ever noticed how some people never see the
2   good in anything? When you talk to them they're always
3   complaining about something. It doesn't matter what you're
4   doing or where you are, these people will find something
5   wrong with their situation. It's almost as if they don't know
6   how to be happy, like they enjoy causing problems and
7   being miserable!

8   I had a friend who was like this. I tried really hard to help
9   her see the good in life, but she would always find a way to
10 turn whatever happened to her into a drama. It got to the
11 point where I had to find myself a new best friend. I just
12 couldn't take the negative atmosphere I was in every time
13 she was around. No matter how hard I tried to lift her up,
14 she ended up bringing me down. I finally decided that it's
15 not healthy being around someone who can do that to you.
16 I made the difficult decision to move on to a different group
17 of friends.

18 Sometimes I wonder if this negative personality trait
19 could be genetic. Do you think that's possible? Or is it an
20 attitude that's learned from the environment these negative
21 people live in? It does seem like whenever you meet a
22 person who's like that, their parents and the rest of their
23 family are, too. So, do they become negative from seeing
24 and hearing their family be that way, or is it something
25 about the way their body is chemically designed that makes
26 them look at things in such a negative way?

27 I know that everyone has times when they feel as if
28 nothing is going right. It's up to us to find out what helps

1   us get out of the negative moods these bad things cause.
2   For me, just listening to the right music can take me out of
3   a bad mood and make me feel better. Exercise is something
4   else I like doing to get rid of any negative energy I'm
5   dragging along. I feel so much better once I've run a few
6   miles or walk on the treadmill. But besides these two things,
7   what helps me more than anything to forget my own
8   problems is helping others with their problems. When you
9   volunteer in the community to help those in need, your
10 problems become pretty small rather quickly.
11   All I know is I don't want to be one of those people who
12 others don't want to be around. Life truly is very short, and
13 we need to live each day to its fullest. There's always
14 someone in this world who has it worse than you, so get over
15 yourself. Make the most of the life you've been given. We can
16 do so much good for others whenever we start looking
17 outside of our own small world. I promise you will start to
18 see the good in life whenever you realize just how blessed
19 all of us in this country are.

Discussion Questions

What suggestions do you have to help negative people become more positive? How are you able to help yourself maintain a positive attitude, even during difficult times? What are your feelings about genetics playing a part in the depressing attitudes some people have?

30. My Mom Is Driving Me Crazy!

1   Why is it that whenever a teenage girl reaches a certain
2 age, her mother starts to drive her crazy?! I know I'm not
3 alone on this matter, I've talked to my friends about this,
4 and they feel the same way. I feel bad about it. I've always
5 been one of the few who get along well with their mom. But
6 lately, it seems that whatever she says rubs me the wrong
7 way!
8   Take last night, for instance. I was going out with some
9 friends and got all dressed up. When I asked Mom how I
10 looked she said, "Well, you look beautiful, of course." That
11 was nice, I thought to myself, but could she stop there? Oh,
12 noooo. She continued by adding, "But I do like your hair
13 better when it's up."
14   If I wear blue, she tells me she likes me better in green.
15 If I have on pants, I should be wearing a dress. If I clean the
16 kitchen, I should have cleaned the bathroom, too. I feel like
17 I never do anything right, I never wear the right things, and
18 I never say what I should say.
19   We were visiting my grandparents on Sunday. Granddad
20 asked what I planned to do with my summer. I told him that
21 I wanted to find a summer job and hopefully have a lot of
22 time to swim in our pool with my friends.
23   I thought that was a good answer, but after we left, I had
24 to listen to my mother go on and on for twenty minutes
25 about how I need to expand upon my ideas further when I'm
26 in conversation with an adult. She wanted to know why I
27 didn't share what kind of jobs I was looking for and perhaps
28 talk a little more about my friends to Granddad. I said, "If

1 Granddad wanted to know more details, he would have
2 asked me!"
3   I've tried talking to her about this. When I shared with
4 her that I didn't think I ever do anything right anymore, she
5 said she feels the same way. She said that no matter what
6 she says or does, I get upset about it. When I was younger,
7 I used to enjoy her sharing her favorite hairstyle or color for
8 me to wear. But now, I just need her to let me make my own
9 decisions.
10   This has really become a problem for us. I want to feel
11 close to my mom again, but it's hard for us to even be
12 around each other right now. Maybe after I leave for college
13 things will get better. We just don't live well together in the
14 same house anymore. Do any of you feel this way?

Discussion Questions

Are any of you able to relate to what our speaker is saying? What is it that mothers and daughters need to understand about each other in order to get along better? When should a mother and daughter try to have a friendship instead of a mother/daughter relationship? Or, should their relationship ever become a friendship?

31. My Best Friend's Getting Married!

1   It is with much regret that I must announce the
2 upcoming wedding ceremony of my best friend. How is that
3 possible? We're only seventeen-years-old! Well, OK, to be
4 honest, Marcy will be eighteen in three months, but
5 honestly, it shouldn't be legal to get married before you're
6 twenty-one!

7   I guess this wedding thing is more or less out of my best
8 friend's hands. Even though she tells me she's cool with the
9 whole marriage thing, I'm still not convinced. You see,
10 Marcy found out two months ago that she's pregnant.
11 According to her parents, marriage is her only option.

12   It's not as if Marcy slept with some guy just for a night
13 of fun or something stupid like that. She's been dating Gary
14 for two years. He's older and went into the service right after
15 high school and Marcy has remained devoted to him ever
16 since. I even tried to get her to double with me and another
17 guy, just as a friend, but no, she didn't want any rumors
18 making their way to Gary and him getting the wrong idea.

19   This serious relationship stuff all happened when Gary
20 came home on leave. After not seeing each other for such a
21 long time, Marcy said things got heated up a little too
22 quickly, and the next month she discovered she was
23 pregnant. She says this certainly isn't the way she wanted
24 things to happen, but now that she's in the middle of this,
25 what else can she do?

26   Personally, I think she's too young to make a promise to
27 Gary that she will remain faithful to him for the rest of her
28 life. Just once, Marcy confided to me that she wondered

1 whether they'd really make it, considering their ages and
2 how he'll be gone so much. But by the next day she'd
3 decided getting married was the best option.
4   How sad it is to have to plan a wedding around a
5 pregnancy. Marcy should be ecstatic about getting married,
6 and be totally consumed in the wedding plans, but I just get
7 this feeling of dread, or something, from her whenever we
8 talk about it.
9   Maybe I'm imagining this, though. I mean, she has so
10 much stress right now — a pregnancy, a marriage, and a
11 high school graduation! I can't help but feel sorry for her. I
12 feel like I'm not being a good friend if I try to talk her into
13 waiting to get married. But on the other hand, how can I
14 stand next to her as her maid of honor knowing that deep
15 inside I disagree with the marriage?
16   I'm not sure whether she truly has a problem with all of
17 this, or if I'm the one with the problem. Marcy and I were
18 supposed to go off to college and room together. Everything
19 we've dreamed about and talked about throughout high
20 school has just gone up in smoke because of this
21 pregnancy. How could Marcy do this to me?
22   *(Pause)* I'm starting to sound really selfish, aren't I?
23 Maybe it is the best thing for Marcy to marry Gary. I mean,
24 people used to get married at sixteen and even younger all
25 the time. She says she loves Gary, too.
26   I just don't know what I'm going to do without my best
27 friend around.

Discussion Questions

If you were in Marcy's position, what would you do?
Should her friend share with Marcy the way she feels about
her upcoming marriage, or should she give Marcy her
blessing and keep quiet? Have you ever kept your feelings to
yourself in order to preserve a friendship?

32. Morality vs. Money

1   Right now one of the most important things my friends
2   and I are trying to do is earn money for college. For the past
3   six months, I've been peddling burgers at the golden arches,
4   and my best friend actually mows grass for her neighbors.
5   After months of performing these tedious tasks, I have
6   accumulated just over one thousand dollars. Sounds like a
7   lot, doesn't it? Until you look at the cost of tuition.

8   I'm not fortunate enough to have parents who are able
9   to pay my way. Whatever I can't save I'll be paying back
10 through my student loan for ten years. Now, let me tell you
11 about the temptation I'm facing.

12   Another one of my friends, Donelle, has found a much
13 simpler way to earn lots of money really fast. She dances.
14 When she first told me that, I didn't get what she was
15 saying. I was like, "What do you mean you earn three
16 thousand dollars a week for dancing? Did you make it to
17 Broadway or something?" That was always her dream, to
18 dance on Broadway.

19   She motioned to me to quiet down, and then she
20 whispered to me what this dancing thing is all about. At
21 first, I couldn't believe it. But now that I've given it some
22 thought, I'm not so sure it's such a bad idea. You see, my
23 friend pole dances at a club in the city. You have to be
24 eighteen, which I am, and be willing to dress rather risqué,
25 which I can do, I guess.

26   My friend said she only has to perform twice a night. Her
27 parents don't know she's doing this. They think she has a
28 job at a coffee house. She said the bar is something *like* a

1 coffee house, and besides, her parents expect her to pay for
2 her own college tuition, too, so why should they decide what
3 she does to earn the money? Donelle made ten thousand
4 dollars in one month. She already has enough money to pay
5 for her first year of school! And here I am, after six months,
6 with only a thousand dollars to show for it.
7   Donelle said she could get my lawn-cutting friend and
8 me jobs dancing. My initial reaction was "No way!" But
9 when Donelle confronted me with "Why not?" the only
10 reason I could think of was it just doesn't seem right. When
11 she replied that she isn't dancing nude, no man is allowed
12 to touch her, and her outfit is just a bit more revealing than
13 her bikini, I started thinking "Why not?"
14   I don't know. The money sure sounds good. Why am I
15 feeling like it's not a good idea then? Maybe I should ask
16 Donelle just how risqué those outfits are. I'm definitely
17 getting tired of the Mickey D's uniform.

Discussion Questions

How do you feel about earning money in ways that are not legally wrong, but are perhaps morally wrong? What plan do you have for earning college money? What words of advice would you have for our actor on how to handle her dilemma?

33. Man's Best Friend

1   No one seems to understand what I'm going through
2 right now. Even my best friends seem to say the wrong
3 thing. I know everyone is just trying to make me feel better,
4 but maybe it would be best if they just said "I'm sorry" and
5 left it at that.
6   You see, my dog died yesterday morning. Her name was
7 Tawny. She was this beautiful collie my parents bought for
8 me when I was two-years-old. Mom once drove me back to
9 the farm where Tawny was born, just so I knew where
10 Tawny came from. It helped me understand how important
11 it was to let Tawny run free in our own fields, and not keep
12 her penned up or tied up with a chain.
13   Collies are herders, so they enjoy being outside, roaming
14 through the wide open spaces. We would take long walks
15 together, and no matter what kind of a day I was having,
16 Tawny would greet me with a wagging tail and a kiss.
17   When I got home from school yesterday, that's exactly
18 how she tried to greet me. She came running out from the
19 barn and when she jumped up to greet me, she just landed
20 on the ground, dead. I couldn't understand what happened.
21 I mean, it was out of the blue. She was just laying on the
22 grass. Then, I realized she wasn't breathing.
23   I know some of you will think it's gross or funny, but I
24 tried to revive her with CPR. I saw that on a TV show once,
25 so I know vets do that. But she never came to. The vet said
26 she had a heart attack, just like a person does. I'm not sure
27 I ever heard of a dog having a heart attack, it never crossed
28 my mind that Tawny could die that way.

1   That dog was the greatest joy in my life. I can't put into
2 words how she could put me in a better mood just by letting
3 me pet her. I told Tawny secrets about myself that I'll never
4 share with a person. It's kind of nice to know that when you
5 share something personal with your pet, you truly can trust
6 them to never tell a soul. Even your best friends seem to
7 have a problem not telling your secret to at least one other
8 person.
9   That's the thing. Tawny was my best friend, and now I
10 feel as if I don't have one. Sure, I have a lot of friends at
11 school, but I don't feel as close to any of them the way I did
12 to Tawny. The thing is, everyone keeps telling me to go get
13 another puppy. Tawny just died yesterday! Do they think
14 she was like a toy that can just be replaced by going to the
15 store and buying a new one? Well, they're wrong. Right now,
16 I'm not sure I want another dog ... ever.
17   *(Pause, thinking)* Do any of you feel this close to your
18 pets? Am I just a crazy person, or am I right to wonder why
19 people don't understand my need to grieve for awhile? Tawny
20 was a living creature who loved me unconditionally, and I've
21 lost that love. Would another dog *really* fill the void I'm
22 feeling?
23   One of my friends said to me, "Look, there are too many
24 people in this world who have dogs and don't deserve them.
25 Now that Tawny is gone, you need to continue sharing your
26 gift of loving animals. Give another dog a new home."
27   Yesterday, I didn't want to hear her words. But now, I'm
28 thinking maybe she's right.

Discussion Questions

How many of you have ever lost a pet you were close to?
Share your stories. Did you get another pet shortly after?
What advantages do you feel an "animal best friend" has
over a "person best friend?"

34. Making the Grade

1   If I have to take one more test I'm going to scream! Do
2 you realize that every day we wake up in this world we are
3 asked to meet some level of criteria? Every direction you
4 turn someone is asking you to reach higher, strive further,
5 and achieve more. When is good enough ever good enough?
6   Don't get me wrong, I'm all about reaching one's
7 potential and doing your best. It's just that I feel as if I can
8 never relax and enjoy what I'm doing. Everything has to be
9 judged or given a grade. Doing something just for
10 enjoyment seems to be an idea from some historical time
11 in our past.
12   Believe it or not, I used to actually like school. But now
13 we have all the tests to take in our classes *and* we have
14 state achievement tests. But before we even take those we
15 have benchmark tests to predict how we'll do on the state
16 achievement tests. Oh, and let's not forget the SATs, and
17 the ACTs.
18   It doesn't stop there. If you're in any type of
19 extracurricular activity, it's always about winning the games
20 and making the playoffs. You can't even join the choir or
21 band anymore without it being about competition and who's
22 the best singer or instrumentalist. I just want to be in
23 something for fun!
24   Take this summer, for instance. I wanted to display
25 some of my art work at the county fair ... until I learned it
26 was all going to be judged with ribbons being awarded. I
27 used to like going to Trivia Club where we studied facts
28 about the county where we live, but even that has turned

1   into a county wide contest.

2   One of these days I'm going to organize some kind of
3   activities for groups where no one is graded, or judged, or
4   scored on how they need to improve. The only criteria
5   needed to be met will be whether or not you had fun
6   participating.

7   Can you even imagine what it would be like to have a
8   class in school where everyone attended just for the sake of
9   great discussion and the sharing of ideas? *(Pause)* You're
10 right, it would probably never work. The idea of competition
11 and being rewarded for hard work is so ingrained in our
12 society's culture that only a few would even attend a class
13 like that.

14   Maybe we should all take up knitting for a hobby. I've
15 heard that's relaxing. *(Pause)* Oh, never mind, everyone
16 would probably want to see who could knit the longest scarf
17 the fastest! Now that might be a fun race to watch!

Discussion Questions

Do you ever feel the same way as this person? Explain.
Why do you think competition is so important in our culture?
What activities are you involved in that don't seem to
include some type of competition? Is it possible for schools
to offer classes where you don't receive a grade? Can sports
be played just for fun?

35. Living in Fear

1   Ever since terrorism touched our homeland many people
2 live in fear of what may happen each day. I admit, on nine-
3 eleven I was truly frightened. You hear of these horrible acts
4 of terrorism happening in other countries, but I never
5 dreamed it would happen here in the United States. I'm sure
6 I will never comprehend how human beings commit such
7 horrendous crimes in the name of their God.

8   I find myself always being leery of foreign people now,
9 which is so unfair to them. All because a group of radicals
10 blew themselves up with thousands of innocent people, I
11 feel differently toward foreigners. I never used to feel
12 prejudice. I didn't see any difference from one person to the
13 next. I'm trying hard not to feel this way, though. I know
14 that the vast majority of those living in our country are loyal
15 citizens devoted to family and their religion. It just makes
16 me angry that terrorism has to play a role in our everyday
17 lives. It saddens me that I once viewed all others as my
18 friends, but now I will not call anyone "friend" until I trust
19 them.

20   On the other hand, why should we in America be the
21 only people in the world who are allowed to live with no fear?
22 There are students in foreign lands who have not even
23 begun to experience what freedom is. We took it for granted.
24 And now that several years have passed since that
25 historical day when thousands of average Americans
26 became heroes, many are once again taking our freedom for
27 granted.

28   Americans of the twenty-first century need to view the

1 world with their rose-colored glasses off their faces. We need
2 to continue the fight, to preserve the freedoms our
3 forefathers so dearly paid the price for us to enjoy. Now it is
4 the turn of our generation to once again sacrifice lives in
5 order to uphold the democratic policies of America — a land
6 for the people, by the people, and of the people.
7   Please don't live in fear or live blindly to the fact that we
8 are vulnerable people. We need to continue to unite as one
9 against terrorism. Nothing else should so strongly connect
10 the countries of the world. I'm sure of one thing: As soon as
11 we let our guard down, the terrorists will let us know they
12 were watching.
13   Let's be thankful for those who choose to spend their
14 lives as leaders for our nation. Whether making daily
15 decisions about policies, or fulfilling a stint overseas as a
16 member of our armed forces, we have a country full of
17 people who we need to be proud of. Let's fight this war on
18 terror and win the battle of fear.

Discussion Questions

What are your opinions about the U.S. involvement in the war against terror? How have your views of the world changed since September 11? Discuss the way many people live in other countries. How are their freedoms different from ours?

36. Let's Hear Some Good News!

1   I'm tired of hearing about all the problems teens today
2 are causing. Every time I turn on the TV there's news about
3 someone my age getting into trouble. I know that lots of
4 teens have problems, but there are also a lot of us trying to
5 live life in a way that makes our parents proud. It just
6 seems as if the news likes to portray our generation as
7 selfish and self-centered. And maybe there's truth to some
8 of that. After all, our generation has been given more
9 material things than any other generation of teens before
10 us.

11   But despite being spoiled, there are a lot of positive
12 things that are also being done by teens today. All you have
13 to do is visit one of the local schools to find out what they
14 are. There are so many clubs and organizations sponsored
15 by the schools that are involved in community services. The
16 group that I'm a part of is dressing up for Halloween and
17 visiting one of the local nursing homes. We're going to play
18 Bingo with the residents and give them cookies we baked.
19 We're all really excited about that afternoon.

20   We also have two blood drives coming up. What's great
21 about those is that the club members have to get other
22 students to volunteer to be donors. By the time we're
23 finished, there will be nearly seventy-five students involved
24 in helping the Red Cross. It's amazing how many of my
25 classmates were willing to donate their blood. I think it
26 really meant something to all of my friends to be a part of
27 the slogan, "Donate blood, save a life." Knowing that we're
28 helping someone else gives us self-worth. It makes us feel

1 like we do have a purpose here. Even with all of the
2 problems we face each day, we are finding ways to do
3 positive things.
4   We're also planning "can dances." That's when your club
5 sponsors a dance and the fee to get in is a can of soup. We
6 take all the cans to the Rescue Mission in town after the
7 dance. Our group will also help at the mission's soup
8 kitchen two times this school year.
9   I'm not trying to brag about our actions. I just want
10 people to know that there are a lot of teens trying to do the
11 right thing. Could someone please send a news reporter to
12 our next event? Let's get the whole truth out to the public.
13 Teenagers really aren't all that bad.

Discussion Questions

What do you do to help your community? Are teenagers
given a bad rap because of the number of teens involved in
reckless behaviors? Devise a list of activities that you and
your friends can organize to help others. Plan how you can
get the word out to your community that your generation is
willing to step up and become concerned citizens who are
investing themselves in the lives of others.

37. Let's Get Fit!

1   I am really worried about our generation. For some
2 reason, so many of us just don't seem to care whether or
3 not we're living healthy. I don't mean to sound like a parent,
4 but it's a little scary to see how many teens sit around for
5 hours and hours in front of a computer or TV screen. It's
6 time for the rest of us to help these teens get physically fit.

7   Some of my friends and I sat around one night thinking
8 of ideas that would make exercising fun. There's a teacher
9 at school who said she would sponsor any activities that we
10 could organize. We decided to hold walkathons to earn
11 homework passes. All we needed to do was get a lot of the
12 teachers to go along with our idea. We were surprised at
13 how many teachers were happy to help us with our exercise
14 plan. The best part about it was that everyone could finish
15 a winner.

16   Each walker has to meet a preset goal determined in
17 gym class by their teacher. If they reach their goal, they
18 receive a free homework pass for a class of their choice. We
19 hold a walkathon once a week, and each week our numbers
20 are increasing. It's becoming one of the cool places to hang
21 out after school, but everyone is getting to exercise at the
22 same time.

23   If you read the statistics on teen obesity, you will
24 understand why we knew we needed to try and be proactive.
25 In a recent report published by the Department of Health
26 and Human Services, it states that fourteen percent of
27 teens are overweight. This number has *tripled* in the last
28 twenty years. If we don't do something now to stop this

1 trend, our country will be facing serious health issues in our
2 younger generations.
3   What we need to realize is that, in the majority of these
4 teens, the condition is preventable. As teenagers, we need
5 to take responsibility for ourselves and make the decision to
6 treat our bodies right.
7   Stop eating junk food and sweets twenty-four-seven,
8 especially when all you're doing is sitting on the couch! I'm
9 sure you've heard of the term *couch potato.* Don't be one!
10   Let's all make a conscious decision today to think of one
11 thing we can do to be proactive in making our generation
12 healthy and fit. It all starts with just one step.

Discussion Questions

What are some ways your school could start up some "Get Fit" exercise programs? How do you maintain your health? Share your own daily plan for staying healthy and fit.

38. Kings and Queens – Who Needs Them?

1   I know what I'm going to say may upset some people,
2 but every year I feel this way and never share my opinion, so
3 ... here it goes. I am so tired of the whole king and queen
4 elections of homecoming and prom. Don't get me wrong, I
5 don't say this because I'm jealous of those who are
6 nominated for these positions. In fact, this is the first year
7 I'm even old enough to be nominated, so it isn't jealousy. I
8 just think the whole idea is stupid.

9   During the time of nominations, everybody suddenly
10 becomes nicer than they usually are. Once the nominations
11 are over with, the finalists become even nicer. Some of the
12 girls are so fake, it makes me want to gag.

13   When I ask people why we still honor such an ancient
14 tradition, they respond, "But that's why we do it, because it
15 *is* tradition." I say, "Let's make new traditions." Instead of
16 doing the same thing year after year, let's make our own
17 mark and come up with our own ideas. Everything else in
18 this world changes, why doesn't the king and queen thing
19 change?

20   Couldn't we just have a special song for all the seniors
21 to dance to during the prom, rather than a select few from
22 the class being called out onto the floor and honored as "the
23 court?" Or maybe we could honor the girl and guy in the
24 class who have performed the most community service
25 hours.

26   Maybe you have some even better ideas. I guess I just
27 think that if two people are going to be held in high esteem
28 by their classmates, it should be about more than just

1 being popular.
2   Tradition is good, I love tradition. But sometimes, it's
3 worthwhile to take a long look at what your traditions are
4 and decide if you've outgrown them. This is one tradition I
5 believe modern day society has moved past.
6   So, I challenge all of you that if you share my opinion
7 about this, get a group from your class together and
8 brainstorm some ideas of your own. See if you're able to
9 create an original celebration that honors all of the special
10 people in your class, not just a select few. Let me know
11 what you come up with. Maybe I can convince some people
12 at my school to make some changes, too.

Discussion Questions

What ways does your class honor students? Do you agree with the old traditions, or would you like to see things change? Besides homecoming and prom elections, what other traditions does your school celebrate? Do you have any ideas for new traditions?

39. It's Graduation Time – What's Next?

1   Here's a question for you — you're only a teenager, just
2 finishing high school, but I'm going to ask you this question
3 anyway — what do you want to do for the rest of your life?
4   Isn't that what you're hearing every time you turn
5 around? If one more person asks me what I'm going to do
6 now that I'm almost finished with high school, I think I'm
7 going to scream! How is a person supposed to know at
8 seventeen what they want to do for the rest of their life!
9   My mom and dad sat me down this past weekend and
10 told me I needed to start thinking about colleges I want to
11 visit. Did they ever think that I might not want to go to
12 college? Maybe I just want to go get a job for a while. I tried
13 explaining this to them, but all they could say back was,
14 "Every person needs a college degree nowadays, if they're
15 ever going to make something of themselves."
16   I guess I'll have to humor them and visit some schools,
17 just to make them happy. What I'd really like to say to them
18 is, "Could I just please have a year to try the world and
19 think about all of this!" I know what they'd say, though, so
20 it's no use even bothering to try and talk to them.
21   At school we took these personality type tests that were
22 supposed to help me see what type of career would suit my
23 personality. I'll be the first to tell you that anything to do
24 with children is out of the question. I do not have the
25 patience for kids. When I get a call to baby-sit, I know the
26 mother calling is at the desperate stage. My name has to be
27 at the bottom of her list. The funny thing is, this test said I
28 might enjoy a job working in a school system. A little

1 ironic, huh? I'm trying to figure that one out!
2   Personally, I think I'd like to work full-time at the stables
3 down the road. I've always loved horses. I could teach riding
4 lessons. Being around the horses makes me feel special. It's
5 like I have this connection, as if they understand how I'm
6 feeling. There's always work to be done there, too. The
7 owner, Rosie, said she'd love to have me work for her.
8   I know I won't get rich working with horses, but I know
9 I'd be happy. It really doesn't matter to me if I make a lot of
10 money. I just need enough to get by. Who knows down the
11 road what could happen. Maybe Rosie would realize how
12 hard I work and give me a manager's position.
13   Oh well, it's a good idea, but that's about all it is. I just
14 don't have the courage to tell my mom and dad, so I guess
15 it's off to college for me.

Discussion Questions

How are you feeling about your future plans after high school? Do you believe it's a good idea for graduates unsure of attending college to just take a year to experience the world? Should you choose your passion over financial security?

40. Is There a Right Kind of Couple?

1　So many times we hear someone say, "Oh, they are the
2　perfect couple!" This makes me start to think about just
3　what *is* a "perfect couple." Is it two people who are
4　inseparable, who do everything together? Or is it more a
5　couple who pursue their own interests, yet come together
6　when they desire a companion? Or maybe it's somewhere in
7　between those two types.

8　All I know is that with the high rate of divorce in today's
9　society, I'd like to figure all of this out sometime before I
10　decide to settle into a relationship. So far, I'm batting zero.
11　I either date guys who want to be with me constantly,
12　suppressing any chance I have for following my own dreams,
13　or I date guys who call whenever they happen to have the
14　urge and leave me wondering why in the world am I going
15　out with them.

16　I've watched my parents' relationship over the years.
17　Theirs seems pretty solid. They definitely have their own
18　interests that the other is not a part of. But anytime I hear
19　Mom or Dad saying, "I'd like to be spending more time
20　together," the next thing I know, they're going out on a date
21　somewhere.

22　My friend's parents recently divorced. She said that they
23　just grew apart, at least that's the reason they gave her for
24　their decision. My question is, "How do you keep growing
25　personally without losing the closeness you and your
26　significant other felt when you first met?" Wouldn't it make
27　sense to say that everyone would grow apart if they
28　continually change from their first encounter?

1   I know some people who seem to stay exactly the same
2 as the years go by. Then there are others, who I associate
3 myself as being similar to, who continue to explore new
4 areas of interest all the time. I feel like I'm a different person
5 every year. I'm always changing and learning new things.
6 But if I'm that kind of person, how will I ever stay connected
7 to a special guy? He'll want the girl he married, and ten
8 years later, maybe even five, or one, I'll be different.
9   Solid relationships that last a lifetime still seem a
10 mystery to me. Maybe I should just ask my mom and dad
11 for advice when the time comes. Wow, did I really say that?
12 Hmmmmph, I guess the two of them are pretty good role
13 models, and I'm just now figuring that out. That's cool, I
14 don't have far to go to find the example of a nearly close to
15 perfect couple. Maybe there is hope for me yet.

Discussion Questions

How would you define a "perfect" couple? When you are
in a relationship, which of the following couple types do you
feel you fit into:

A. independent thinkers

B. an inseparable twosome

C. companionship seekers only

Explain how you think some couples' relationships last a
lifetime.

41. Is Our Family Falling Apart?

1   I never expected to see what I saw last Saturday night.
2 In fact, I've been wishing every free moment I have that I'd
3 never witnessed any of it. That I was still clueless. That I
4 could just pretend I didn't know my mom is having an
5 affair. If I hadn't seen it play out before my very own eyes, I
6 would deny it was true. Anyone who knows my mom
7 wouldn't believe it either.

8   But it is true. I saw her with another man when I went
9 out Saturday night. She told us she was meeting her
10 girlfriend at the movies, a chick flick my dad wouldn't want
11 to see. So, who would question her? No one would ask her
12 about the movie later. No one would really care if it was any
13 good, even though one of us might actually have asked,
14 "How was it?" That would be the extent of our interest in it.
15 I have to admit, good alibi, Mom. But it was an awful,
16 disgusting thing to do to us! How could you?!

17   My dad is a great guy. He's always there for us any time
18 we need him. He's never missed a day of work in the past
19 twenty years. We sit in church together as a family every
20 Sunday morning. What a hypocrite my mother is! What a
21 joke our family is! If I saw her, I'm sure someone else did,
22 too. How many people know about this besides me?

23   Right now I'm feeling embarrassed, angry, and
24 frustrated all at one time. Is that even possible? I just want
25 to run through the streets screaming! I can't even put into
26 words how I feel. And now, I don't know what to do.

27   Should I tell my dad? Should I let my mom know her
28 secret is out? I can't keep it if she asks me to. I could never

1   do that to my dad. But if I tell him, won't that just hurt him?
2   I don't want to be the one to share that kind of information
3   with him. That's not something a child should have to tell
4   their parent.
5   Don't think I've jumped to conclusions, either. Believe
6   me, it was obvious there was something going on between
7   my mother and her "friend." Friends don't join in a lip-lock
8   that lasts a whole minute, or longer!
9   Part of me wants to push the moment back to a place in
10 my brain where I will never think of it again. But another part
11 of me wants our family to heal. It sounds so weird saying
12 that, because three days ago, I didn't know we had any
13 problems to work out. Now, it seems as if my whole life is a
14 problem. I don't even know what's real anymore.
15   As mad as I am at my mom right now, I love her so
16 much. I just need to know why she would do this. I can't let
17 my family fall apart.

Discussion Question

In this situation, what do you feel is the best action for this young lady to take? Are there ever circumstances when you believe it's OK for a married person to have an affair? What about boyfriend/girlfriend relationships? At what point do you believe a person must stay true to only one other person? Have you ever cheated or been cheated on? What do you think could prevent this from happening?

42. Is It Ever OK to Lie?

1   This morning I ran into my best friend right after she
2 had an appointment at her salon. I'm not sure what they did
3 to her hair, but personally, I think it looks awful! I hesitated
4 for a moment when I first saw her, doing a double take to
5 make certain it was even her. Then, when she asked, "How
6 do you like it?" I lied and said it looked great. Afterward, I
7 wondered if that was the right thing to do. I mean, we're
8 always told to be honest, but if your best friend isn't honest
9 with you, who can you trust to tell the truth?

10   I've also been taught to not hurt other people's feelings.
11 Don't you think my friend would have been terribly hurt if I
12 told her I didn't like her new hairdo? All of this leads me to
13 the question, "Is it ever OK to lie?"

14   I've learned at Christmas time to be ready with the "I
15 just love this!" face whenever I open up what Grandma
16 gives me. I know she spends a lot of time and money on all
17 of us grandkids, and the last thing I would ever want to do
18 is to make her feel bad. So, when I open her gifts, I just
19 pretend I love them. Then, I usually make up an excuse, like
20 it's too small, or I have something similar to it, in order to
21 return the gift to the store. Is it OK to lie to my grandma in
22 that way?

23   It never used to bother me to lie in order to spare
24 another's feelings. I always thought that justified lying, but
25 lately I've been second guessing this theory. It seems like
26 I'm always saying what other people think I *should* say,
27 instead of what I'm truly thinking or feeling.

28   Even in class there are times when the teacher asks us

1   to say how we feel about certain issues. The topics are
2   usually debatable, and two sides are discussed. If I know
3   which stance the teacher believes in, I find myself saying
4   that's how I feel, just so the teacher thinks I'm an OK
5   person. I'm afraid he or she might not give me an A in the
6   class if I say things against the way they believe.
7   I've also lied to fit in with the crowd. If everyone decides
8   they want to go to a certain place to eat after a game, I'll
9   say that's great, even if I'd much rather go somewhere else.
10 I just don't like to rock the boat, so to speak. The more I
11 think about this, I sound like a habitual liar! What is wrong
12 with me? Can I not think for myself and say out loud how I
13 feel?
14   This is a problem I have got to work out. Just tell me,
15 do you think it's ever OK to lie?

Discussion Questions

Answer the question presented by the actor: Is it ever
OK to lie? Share examples of times you believe it may be
OK to tell a lie. If you feel one should not ever lie, how would
you handle situations so as not to hurt another's feelings?
Would you want to be lied to? If someone didn't like your
new shirt, or new haircut, would you want them to tell you?

43. Is He Worth It?

1　It has been such a long time since I have met anyone
2　even remotely interesting. I almost gave up hope on ever
3　finding a guy who was attractive, yet able to carry on a
4　conversation for more than a minute. Thankfully, last month
5　I met him, the guy who is great looking, intelligent, and
6　seems interested in me as a person. He actually does exist,
7　and I can't believe that I met him!

8　I've tried meeting nice guys at football games, parties,
9　you name it. My friends from other schools would hook me
10　up with some guys who they thought were nice. It just never
11　seemed to work out. Until last month ...

12　Mom asked me to go to the library and pick up my little
13　brother from the preschool story hour. He's only three and
14　he thinks he's really big stuff when he gets to go to the
15　library with his friends. While I was waiting for him in the
16　lobby, I kept trying to call my friend on my cell phone. I was
17　getting really frustrated because I had no service. On about
18　my fifth try, Mark, that's his name, came over and offered
19　me his phone to use. I thought to myself, "How sweet!"

20　When I finished my phone call, Mark and I started
21　talking. We went on and on as if we'd known each other for
22　years instead of minutes. When the little kids came out, he
23　asked if I'd mind giving him my number. I took his phone
24　again and said I'd be glad to add it to his contact list.
25　Honestly, I wanted to make sure he didn't lose it or forget it.

26　Everything to this point sounds like a dream come true,
27　right? Well, we all know dreams don't really come true, at
28　least not the way we imagine. Mark and I have spent a lot

1   of time together over the past month. He likes to do things
2   outdoors like I do. We've been biking at the park, canoeing,
3   we even went snorkeling at the beach.

4   Just when I thought things couldn't get any better, he
5   dropped a bomb on me. I knew something was up when he
6   said we needed to talk, that there was something really
7   important he had to tell me and it couldn't wait any longer.

8   When Mark shared his little secret with me, he tried to
9   add a bit of humor to it. He told me that he had another
10 girlfriend. Believe me, I wasn't laughing. I could feel my
11 stomach getting sick, but I just let him keep talking. He
12 said she was the love of his life and that I'd actually met her
13 one time.

14   Then Mark pulled out a picture of the little girl he picked
15 up from the library the day we met. He said he waited to tell
16 me about her until he was sure we were going to be
17 something special as a couple, and I needed to know
18 everything about him. He has a three-year-old little girl.

19   Wow! Talk about feeling as if you ran into a brick wall.
20 Now I have to decide if he's really worth it. We're only
21 seniors in high school. Do I really want to continue in this
22 relationship, knowing the responsibilities Mark already has?
23 I just don't know.

Discussion Questions

Would you be able to handle dating a high school guy who already had a child? What would you do in this person's position? Should Mark have told her sooner about his child, or was he right in saying that he needed to make sure the relationship was working before he shared that information? If this were you, what questions would you need answered in order to help you make a decision about continuing this relationship?

44. Is Assisted Suicide Moral?

1   Last summer I sat by my dog's side while the vet
2 dripped medicine into her, which caused her to pass away
3 without pain. As sad as I was, I have to admit, I felt peace
4 when it was all over. My dog was suffering, and to be able
5 to hold her close while she took her last breath was
6 comforting. I felt that I was with her to the very end.

7   That experience made me start wondering. Would it be
8 OK to allow people who are suffering to die such a painless
9 death? I know it's a questionable issue. I'm just trying to
10 decide how I feel about it. I mean, if the person knows they
11 have an incurable disease and they're living in constant
12 pain, is it wrong to allow them the right to choose to die?

13   But, what if, right after the doctor gives the person the
14 medicine, which will cause their death, that person has a
15 change of heart? Can you stop the process and say, "Hey!
16 Wait a minute! I decided to put up with this pain a little
17 longer! I just remembered my granddaughter is graduating
18 from preschool next week, and I'd like to be there!" Are you
19 able to do that, because don't you think in at least one case
20 that might happen?

21   Sometimes the argument for assisted suicide is that
22 people no longer have any quality to their lives. People say
23 that they shouldn't have to live a lifestyle different from
24 what they've lived all their lives. I guess that sounds like a
25 valid argument, but then I think of the famous actor,
26 Christopher Reeves. You know who I mean, he played
27 Superman in the 70s. Now there's a perfect example of a
28 man who suffered a tragic loss in his physical abilities. No

1 doubt, the quality of life he was used to changed
2 dramatically, but the courage he displayed in living on was
3 heroic. I believe he made a lifelong impact on mankind
4 during the years following his accident. What a loss the
5 human race would have suffered had Christopher Reeves
6 chosen to die.
7   I'm just not a hundred percent decided about how I feel
8 on this issue. I don't think I would ever choose to die, even
9 if I were terminally ill and suffering, but do I have a right to
10 say that others shouldn't make that choice? I don't know. I
11 may be thinking about this one for a long time.

Discussion Questions

Should a person with a terminal illness, living in constant pain, be allowed to choose death? Explain why you feel the way you do about this topic.

45. In with the Old, Out with the New

1   I've been brought up to appreciate the simple things in
2 life. My family has never had a lot of money, but I've never
3 needed anything I didn't have. We've just always found
4 happiness in spending time together, doing things like
5 camping, fishing, and playing board games. Yeah, I know, it
6 sounds dorky, but actually, we're a pretty tight-knit family
7 that a lot of my friends wish they were a part of.

8   Sometimes my friends ask me why it is that my family
9 gets along so well and enjoys being together. Well, when I
10 say what I'm about to say, I know I'm going to sound pretty
11 old, but here it goes anyway ... just what is it with all this
12 technological stuff? If people want to understand why it is
13 that no one spends time with each other anymore, take a
14 clue by looking around you.

15   My guess is that nine out of every ten drivers I see go by
16 are talking on their cell phones. Even when you are with a
17 friend, if that cell phone rings, the majority of people will
18 ignore who they're with and answer their phone. Don't get
19 me wrong, I have a cell phone, but I really try to use good
20 manners when I'm with others, like not answering it! They'll
21 call back or leave a message!

22   When my family takes a road trip, we enjoy that time in
23 the car together, catching up on what's going on in our
24 lives. During a vacation I took with my friend's family, every
25 person in the car, except the driver, had on their own set of
26 earphones to their own iPods so not one word was shared
27 between anyone!

28   Some of my friends would rather spend their entire night

1   at the computer, just in case a guy they like happens to get
2   online. If I hang out with a friend, they still want to be
3   hooked into the computer, just in case ... how do they think
4   that makes me feel? I may as well go home and spend time
5   with someone who wants to see me.

6   Even the cable networks provide entertainment for you
7   twenty-four-seven. So why would people take the time to
8   organize picnics or swim parties to get together when all
9   they have to do is push a button to get in touch with
10 someone else?

11   When my friends and I do get together, we're often
12 circled around a big old bonfire roasting marshmallows,
13 talking and laughing while some music is playing on the
14 radio. Do people realize you can actually live longer from
15 laughing every day? If they did, they'd probably throw out all
16 their techno stuff, quit communicating by wire and air
17 waves, and start having fun by spending time together.

18   Try taking a look at your own family and friends and see
19 if you could make some simple changes to get closer to each
20 other. It might not be easy at first, but it will definitely be
21 worth the effort.

Discussion Questions

Do teens overuse technology? Do you? What are some activities you do that do not involve technology in some way? How does your family handle a road trip? Would you be willing to give up your cell phones, computers, TV, etc., for one week just to see how you would fill your time?

46. I Had a Bad Day!

1   I knew this day was going to be trouble when I woke up
2 an hour late. Don't ask me what I was thinking about while
3 I set my alarm last night, but something had me distracted.
4   I rushed around like an idiot trying to get to school
5 before 10:30, or else I wouldn't get to play in my basketball
6 game tonight. Well, you guessed it. I walked into the office
7 at 10:36, and do you think they'd cut me a little slack? Of
8 course not, the secretary marked me tardy and sent an
9 ineligibility slip down to the coach! I tried everything to get
10 her to bend a little. Nothing worked. I tried tears, humor,
11 even the idea that the school's clocks are fast! I am still
12 furious with that lady.
13   I had to walk into the middle of math class where they
14 were taking a test. My teacher made me start the test,
15 which was not a big deal, except for the fact that I didn't
16 have time to finish it, and he expected me to come back
17 during my study hall to get the test done. You ask, "Why is
18 that a problem?" It's a problem because I needed my study
19 hall to get my English homework done for the next period!
20 So, now I got a bad mark in English for not having my work
21 done.
22   After school, my mom's friend hired me to baby-sit her
23 little boy for a few hours. I finally thought my day was
24 getting back to normal. I took the little boy outside to play
25 ball for awhile, and we had a great time. But when we went
26 to go back inside the house, I somehow managed to lock us
27 out! So, there I am with a four-year-old little boy, who has
28 to pee, no key, and no phone. How could I be so stupid?

1   Luckily, a neighbor was outside and she let me borrow
2 her phone and use her bathroom. I called my mom, who
3 came and got me and the little boy. We left a note on the
4 door of the house, so Mom's friend would know we were now
5 at my house. Mom said to just relax, that things like this
6 can happen to anybody. I just feel like I look so
7 irresponsible! I wonder if her friend will ever ask me to baby-
8 sit again?

9   Then I endured the hour of sitting the bench during my
10 basketball game, while my coach gave me the evil glare now
11 and again for being late and making me ineligible. Our team
12 lost by two points, so of course, I feel as if it's my fault we
13 lost. I usually average ten points a game, so I'm sure Coach
14 thought we wouldn't have lost if I had only been responsible
15 about getting to school on time.

16   You would think I had been put through enough by now,
17 but my friend just called to tell me my boyfriend is planning
18 on breaking up with me. That's nice. At this point in the
19 day, I'm not even sure if I care. It's almost time for bed now,
20 so I'm hoping and praying that tomorrow will be a better
21 day.

22   I just keep telling myself that even though today is a day
23 I'd love to forget, I'm still livin', I'm still healthy, and things
24 could be worse. So, I'm going to try to stay positive.
25 Tomorrow's always another day. Right?

Discussion Questions

Share some of your own bad day experiences. Tell how you were able to cope with it all. Are you able to think of any ways you can help prevent a bad day from occurring?

47. I Feel Like a Mom

1   I'd like to take a survey among teenagers. How many of
2 you out there are expected to work around the house and
3 baby-sit your younger brothers "just because you're a part
4 of the family?" That's the line I hear from my mom and dad
5 every day, and to be quite frank, I'm getting tired of it.

6   Let's be honest. I really don't mind doing some work
7 around the house. Cleaning my own room and washing my
8 own dishes is fine. I made the mess, I'll clean it. But that's
9 not what my parents think.

10   My mom says she does the cooking, so I can do the
11 cleaning up after dinner. Where is the fairness in that? I am
12 one person in a family of six. Why should I have to clean all
13 those dishes by myself? Well, all right, we *do* have a
14 dishwasher.

15   I have three younger brothers. For some reason they
16 don't have to do any work in the kitchen. My dad came from
17 a pretty old-fashioned family where men and women had
18 two sets of standards. Women do all the housework and the
19 men do all the outside jobs, like mowing the grass and
20 washing the cars. Does anybody care that I *love* to be
21 outside? I would swap cleaning the bathrooms and
22 scrubbing pots and pans any day for a job in the fresh air.
23 Don't tell me to ask my parents about a job trade — I've
24 already tried it. No deal.

25   Here's another complaint I'll lay on you. My parents
26 bought me an old, used car. The car is not my complaint. It
27 might be old, but it works. That's all that matters to me.
28 The problem is I have to drive my brothers all over the place

1   for my parents. I'm so tied up taking the boys to ball
2   practice and band that I never have free time to enjoy the
3   car myself!
4   Mom and Dad say that I'm being selfish when I talk this
5   way. I guess it might sound like that to an outsider, but to
6   my friends who really know what I'm going through, think I
7   sound like a mother! I'm too young for all of this! Ugh!

Discussion Questions

What do you feel is a fair amount of responsibility when you are part of a family? How much help should be expected of an older sister in relation to the child care of her siblings? Share what jobs you do in your household to help. Are you paid for doing chores, or is this considered a family responsibility?

48. I Don't Want to Move!

1   Last night I found out that my mom and dad are
2 planning for our family to move across the country at the
3 end of this school year! Next year will be my senior year!
4 How could they even think that this would be OK with me?
5 I have been going to the same school, with the same
6 friends, since kindergarten! I can't even look at either of my
7 parents right now.

8   My little sister only makes matters worse. She's in
9 seventh grade. "This is going to be awesome," she says,
10 and "I can't wait to meet all the new people." I want to
11 reach out and strangle her when she starts. She only makes
12 me look bad because I keep reminding my parents about
13 how unbelievably unfair this whole moving idea is, and they
14 keep telling me to act a little more mature like my sister!
15 Don't they realize how different it is for a seventh grader to
16 move compared to me, who will be a senior?!

17   I guess I understand why my parents had to make this
18 decision. My dad's company is down-sizing and the only way
19 he can keep his job is to change locations. I just wonder
20 why he can't move there by himself for one school year until
21 I'm graduated. Maybe by then I can enroll in college and be
22 set to live on my own here, even if they do move away.

23   I've also been thinking about asking one of my friends if
24 I could move in with them for the year. I've heard of other
25 families allowing that. I'm just not sure if any of my friends'
26 parents would be up for it. I could try begging and crying.
27 That might work.

28   To be honest, though, I can't imagine living with another

1   family instead of my own. And if I'm really truthful, I have to
2   admit that there are times I wonder what it would be like to
3   go to a different school. Maybe I'm just comfortable with the
4   way life has been. Maybe I should be more open to trying
5   new things and meeting new people.
6   My parents said the new school is twice as big as my
7   school now. That really scares me, but it also excites me. In
8   a school that big, there's a lot offered to the students that I
9   don't have now. One thing is a swimming team. I swim for
10 our YWCA now, but at our new home I could actually swim
11 for the school. There would be tons of kids to meet, but on
12 the other hand, it sounds so big that I'm afraid no one would
13 even notice me.
14   Ugh! Why do I even have to be in this position? I like my
15 life just the way it is. Let's face it, I am a creature of habit
16 and that's the way I like it. But it seems like there's one
17 thing in life you can always count on — change. No matter
18 what decision I make, my life is going to be different. I'm
19 just not sure if I can deal with it.

Discussion Questions

If you were facing a move before your senior year, how would you feel about it? Could you move in with a friend or relative and be happy? What do you feel you would be giving up by leaving your home and school for your senior year? Would you have the same things in your new school? How would you make this situation work for you?

49. Homeless

1   I never thought I'd have to say this about my family, but
2 as of last month, we are homeless. I'm really still in shock
3 about it. I knew my parents were having trouble financially.
4 Dad lost his job last year and his unemployment benefits
5 were running out. Mom only gets paid minimum wage
6 working as a sales clerk, so things were getting tight. There
7 were so many times I offered to get a part-time job, but Dad
8 insisted I'd ruin my chances for a college scholarship if I did
9 that. Now I'm feeling really guilty about not helping my
10 parents keep our house.

11   I went to the guidance counselor today and talked to her
12 about everything. She tried to tell me that the little bit of
13 extra money from a part-time job would not make a
14 difference when it comes to mortgages. But I think if I had
15 contributed something, no matter how small, at least I
16 wouldn't have these awful feelings of guilt to deal with.

17   Right now we're living in my grandparents' basement.
18 They said we can stay there as long as we need to, but,
19 obviously, it's not easy living here. Don't get me wrong, my
20 grandparents are two of the best people I know in this
21 world, but they are of a different generation and don't
22 exactly understand me. I'm not sure if they ever realized
23 that their little granddaughter grew up. Last night they
24 asked me if I should be in bed since it was a school night.
25 It was eight o'clock!

26   When my boyfriend came over we had to sit up on the
27 couch without any part of our bodies touching. We were
28 trying to watch a show, but when my grandparents walked

1 through the room and noticed a guy and girl making out on
2 the show, they sent my mother in to let us know the show
3 was inappropriate. I guess I'll solve that problem by always
4 going to my boyfriend's house to see him, instead of him
5 coming to mine.
6   I keep telling my parents that if we could even get a
7 small apartment, I would be happier. But right now, I guess
8 we don't even have enough money to afford that on our own.
9 *(Sigh)* I still think I'm going to find a job. It might not help
10 much, but it can't possibly hurt.

Discussion Questions

Do you ever consider the possibility of your family losing their home? Explain. How would you feel about moving in with relatives? Are there any whom you feel you could actually get along with, if you lived with them? What steps would you take to help, if you were in this girl's position?

50. Has This Purity Thing Gone Too Far?

1   All right, we all have our own personal opinions on
2 premarital sex. Ever since the fifth grade we've been
3 learning about abstinence and safe sex in health class. It's
4 like the school is making sure they don't step on any
5 parents' toes, so they teach us both opinions and let us
6 make up our own minds. Actually, the teachers are told to
7 tell us that abstinence is always the best choice, but *if* you
8 decide to go ahead and try it, then here's the safe way to go
9 about it.

10   That's cool. I understand that. It's just that lately I've
11 been seeing so much advertising about staying pure and
12 signing purity contracts that things seem to be going a bit
13 overboard. I mean, I think I may be one of the few teenagers
14 who believe we should wait until we're married to have sex.
15 But I'm not sure I need to hold up a billboard and tell the
16 world my feelings about it.

17   A few of my friends are wearing purity rings and signing
18 contracts about staying pure. They keep asking me about
19 doing that, too. I just don't get why we need to make a
20 show of our belief system. If that's what they believe, then
21 fine. But it's almost like they're waving their virginity in
22 everyone else's faces. Do you really need to let everyone in
23 on your personal decisions in life? It only seems to make
24 other people think my friends feel they're better than them.
25 Sort of the holier-than-thou type. And from what I can tell,
26 that doesn't seem to sway anyone to your beliefs. In fact, it
27 turns people off.

28   In my hometown, they're holding a purity ball. All the

1   young girls and guys who attend actually wear white and
2   sign papers pledging their purity until marriage. Their
3   parents witness the event and sign the papers, too. I guess
4   I just wonder what it makes those young people feel like if
5   they change their minds later in life. Do they have a
6   tremendous sense of guilt to deal with because they broke
7   the promise they made when they were thirteen years old?
8   Personally, I've made up my own mind to stay celibate
9   until I'm married. But I don't plan to profess it to the
10 masses. It's a belief I have that's tucked in my heart. I pray
11 that I'm able to stay true to it, because I do think that's one
12 of the most special gifts you can honor the man you love
13 with on your wedding day. But it's not my place to judge
14 anyone else who makes a different decision than mine about
15 sex. No matter what your beliefs are about premarital sex,
16 the impact of such a personal relationship with someone
17 else can last a lifetime. We all need to be very careful about
18 making this decision.

Discussion Questions

If you are comfortable in sharing your belief system regarding premarital sex, please share this with others in your group. What lifelong effects do you feel happen when you choose to engage in sex before marriage? What are the dangers of casual sex? Should your parents be involved in any way when you're making decisions about sex? Is it OK to share your personal, intimate choices with your best friends? Would you mind if your boyfriend shared your relationship details with his friends?

5 I. Has Freedom Gone Too Far?

1   Just the other day I heard a famous person on the radio
2 making derogatory remarks about our country's former
3 president. Now, I realize that everyone is entitled to their
4 own opinion, but there is this line of respect, which even I
5 know is not proper to cross. Sometimes I start to think that
6 the founding fathers would not be happy with the extent to
7 which we have allowed freedom to reign.

8   When they wrote "freedom of speech," did they mean
9 that we're allowed to publicly denounce the elected leader of
10 our country? A sense of humor is one thing, but should
11 someone be allowed to make fun of the former vice
12 president for an accidental shooting of his friend while
13 hunting? Some things just shouldn't be turned into jokes.

14   On a smaller scale, I can't believe what students can get
15 away with. There was once a kid who wrote a rap song
16 about a teacher. His lyrics included threats directed at the
17 teacher and the teacher's family. When the school took
18 action against the kid, he sued the school district, saying
19 his freedom of speech was being violated, and he won the
20 case! Is that the freedom the historical figures of
21 Revolutionary War times were talking about when they
22 proclaimed that men should be allowed to speak their
23 opinions freely and openly?

24   Last month, I witnessed protesters burning the
25 American flag openly, while denouncing the war. Ever since
26 I was old enough to come to school I have stood and
27 pledged my allegiance to the flag and my country. Now, I
28 have to watch fellow Americans burn one of our beloved

1   symbols, all in the name of freedom.
2   A lot of people are saying the government has too many
3   rights. I recently read a detailed article discussing the
4   Secret Service listening in on people's conversations in
5   order to prevent terrorism. The citizens are irate, claiming
6   the president and his colleagues had no right to invade
7   another's privacy in this way. I admit, it is a little unnerving
8   to think that someone could be listening in on my
9   conversations. But let's be honest, after one minute of
10 hearing me talk with my friends about the guys in my class,
11 the upcoming dance, and the best color for my prom dress,
12 I don't have to worry about the government wanting to listen
13 in on my conversations for very long. If you're not discussing
14 anything illegal, what do you have to worry about? How do
15 these protesters expect the government to intercept
16 terrorist plots if we don't give them the freedom to perform
17 undercover tasks?
18   All I know is that Washington and Jefferson would not be
19 happy.

Discussion Questions

Just how much freedom of speech do you feel we, as Americans, should have? When do you feel our freedom of speech is taken too far? Discuss the examples our actor presented: derogatory remarks about our country's leaders, threatening remarks about a school teacher and their family, burning the American flag, and phone lines being bugged. What is your opinion on each of these activities?

52. Hands Off! He Was Mine!

1   I would like someone to clarify for me exactly what the
2 "hands-off" policy of dating is, because I'm afraid I'm very
3 confused. Just when is it OK to date a guy who was
4 someone else's boyfriend? Or, how about a guy that one of
5 your friends has been crushing on for the past four years,
6 but it's quite clear he will never like her as more than a
7 friend? Is it OK to go out with him if he decides he's
8 interested in you?
9   It seems like more and more guys are "off-limits" as my
10 high school years go by. Frankly, I'm getting sick of it. Take
11 last week. This really cool senior asked me out. We met
12 during the summer and have been talking ever since. Well,
13 one of my friends has had a crush on him since junior high,
14 but he's never returned the interest. She found out that I
15 was going to the movies with him and won't even speak to
16 me anymore. Not only is she ignoring me, but she's
17 convinced three other girls to boycott me, too. What's this
18 all about? It's not like I purposely went after a guy I knew
19 she wished would talk to her. It just happened that way.
20   Oh yeah, here's another situation one of my friends is
21 in. She used to be best friends with this girl, but they
22 haven't even seen each other for the past nine months. The
23 girl moved to a neighboring school district, and even though
24 my friend tried to keep in touch with this girl, her friend
25 never returned her phone calls. It was as if the girl had
26 made a new life for herself and moved on.
27   Anyway, my friend started dating the other girl's ex-
28 boyfriend. Those two had been a couple for a long time,

1 nearly three years, so their breakup was a big deal around
2 here. Everyone thought they would be the high school
3 sweethearts who ended up married ... but they didn't.
4 So, once my friend started dating this guy, the old
5 girlfriend showed up at her door, ranting about how could
6 she do this to her when they were best friends for so many
7 years. She couldn't believe my friend would cross over the
8 line this way. She told my friend that they could never be
9 friends again.
10 My friend just looked at her and said, "I didn't know we
11 were *still* friends. I haven't talked to you since last
12 September, and anytime I tried to call you, you never
13 returned my call."
14 Do you see what I'm saying now? I just don't know how
15 long this guy was supposed to be "off-limits."
16 There are times I think life would be much easier if I just
17 forgot about guys. I mean, who really needs them? *(Pause,*
18 *thinking)* I do! Let's face it, life's a whole lot more fun with
19 guys around!

Discussion Questions

What seems to be the "hands-off" policy you and your
friends follow when it comes to guys? How do you feel about
the two situations our actor discussed? Would you have
dated the guy involved in each situation? How do you feel
about dating two guys at the same time? Would it be OK
with you if a guy dated you and another girl at the same
time?

53. Guys + Girls = Confusion

1   Will somebody *please* explain guys to me ... if you can.
2 Ever since I started dating, my life seems like a continuous
3 roller coaster! One week I'm riding high, thrilled with the
4 relationship I'm in, and ka-boom! Things come crashing
5 down before I even know what's happened.
6   My most recent boyfriend seemed like the perfect match
7 for me. We both play basketball, we both love to swim, and
8 it was fun when we hung out together. I thought everything
9 was going great. We even went out for a special dinner and
10 a movie the night before he went on vacation just so we
11 could spend every last minute together before he left.
12   You know what's coming next, don't you? Well, you're
13 right. He cheated on me the entire time he was away. I
14 guess his family vacations at the same beach every year,
15 and he has this girl he's met there since he was thirteen!
16 They were all over each other for two entire weeks, while I
17 was sitting at home watching reruns of *Saved By the Bell* for
18 the hundredth time in my life!
19   I found all of this out through a friend who also
20 happened to be vacationing at the same beach as him. I
21 guess he even tried bribing her with money not to tell me.
22 He actually told my friend that it wasn't any big deal, it's
23 only a summer fling he looks forward to each year, and he
24 does really love me. He said it was going to be her fault if I
25 got hurt, because I should never even know about his little
26 rendezvous.
27   Does that confuse you a little bit, because it sure has
28 me confused! How can you be in love with someone and

1 truly believe that being with another person is not hurting
2 the one you love? Does he not realize that I'm not blind? It's
3 not as if I don't see other attractive guys and think they
4 might be fun to go out with. But I never would, not if I'm in
5 love with another guy, or even just dating another guy. It's
6 called respecting the other person.
7   I don't know. I'm not sure I have the time for all of this
8 drama in my life right now. I think I might put all guys on
9 hold until I'm out of school. Right now, they all seem too
10 immature for me. Maybe when I'm ... oh, I don't know,
11 twenty-five, I'll start looking around again. Until then, I'll
12 just keep shooting the basketball and swimming laps. That
13 makes life much less confusing, don't you agree?

Discussion Questions

If you knew someone was cheating on another person, would you tell that person? Is there ever a time when you think it would be OK not to tell? Did you ever find yourself in the position of meeting a great guy on vacation while you're already in a relationship? In your opinion, what would be appropriate behavior if you were in this position?

54. Growing Apart

1   I feel as if I don't even know my best friend anymore.
2 Oh, don't worry, it's not that we had a fight or that she's
3 into drugs, nothing like that. It's more like this gradual
4 change that's been happening ever since we entered high
5 school.
6   Angie and I were always inseparable. We always liked
7 the same things and wanted to go to the same places. We
8 even ate the same goofy sandwiches — peanut butter,
9 mayonnaise, and pickles! But it's finally hit me this year
10 that we are just not the same people anymore. It's really
11 sad, and I'm hating it.
12   When I talked to my mom about it, she said it's natural
13 for friends to grow apart as they get older. Angie made
14 cheerleading, and I'm more into sports. Our schedules are
15 so different, that it's hard for us to make time to get
16 together. When we do have the same free time, Angie is
17 usually invited to a party the other cheerleaders are going
18 to, or I have something to do with my teammates.
19   Like I said, this is really weird to me. I never thought
20 Angie and I would grow distant. And it's not like we want it
21 to be that way, it just is. We keep trying to make our
22 friendship last, but lately it's hard to even come up with
23 things we both want to talk about. She's not interested in
24 going to watch an away game on the weekend. Angie is
25 more interested in going to parties and cruising around town
26 checking out the guys. Which, don't get me wrong, I like to
27 look at a good-looking guy, but I have no interest in
28 spending all night just driving around town in a circle

1 waving at guys. I'd rather go watch them playing ball!
2   How do you stop being best friends with someone who's
3 been there for you since kindergarten? I'm just not ready to
4 give up our friendship yet. I wish things could go back to the
5 way they were when life was less complicated, and all we
6 had to worry about was playing on the swing set and getting
7 home on time for supper.
8   Well, we both still like to go shopping, and of course,
9 we'll never stop enjoying a pizza together. So, maybe I
10 should give her a call and keep trying to get together. I
11 guess friendship is no different than any other type of
12 relationship. Sometimes it takes a little work to keep it
13 going. It's just a hard thing to admit when you thought
14 you'd be best friends forever.

Discussion Questions

What do you think makes a friendship endure through all the changes high school presents? What is it that you and your best friends have in common? Can you think of friendships you had in elementary or middle school which didn't last? What changes caused you to no longer be close to a friend? Do you have a "forever friend" now? What is it that makes your friendship so special?

55. Good and Bad Choices

1   Don't you wish we had a crystal ball to look into the
2   future? It could tell us what's going to happen after we
3   make our choices. Life would be much easier, and I wouldn't
4   be stuck trying to figure out how I'm going to get out of half
5   of the messes I get myself into.
6   It seems that in high school we're always faced with
7   hundreds of choices, almost daily. Sometimes it's really
8   easy to know what to do, but many times, I'm not really
9   sure what's the best decision. I've been making some pretty
10 bad choices lately, and I'm determined to get things turned
11 around in my life.
12   Last week, I had so much trouble getting up in the
13 mornings. I was late for school three out of the five days! I
14 didn't think it was a big deal, until the principal told me I
15 was getting a Saturday detention the next time I was late.
16 Well, I work on Saturdays, so I'd have to call off of work.
17 That *would* be a big deal. My boss has no tolerance for
18 people who call off. If I'm late again, I'll not only be in
19 trouble at school, but also at work! I have got to find an
20 alarm clock that wakes me up!
21   Yesterday, I went shopping after school. I knew Mom
22 told me to be home by six o'clock for supper, but there were
23 such great buys I just had to stay and check them all out.
24 Sure enough, it was six before I knew it. I was home by six-
25 thirty, but Mom was furious at me. She had cooked a really
26 nice meal and was trying to have a family dinner while Dad
27 was in town. He travels a lot, so sitting down together for
28 supper only happens once in awhile. Anyway, she held

1   supper as long as she could, but she was disappointed in
2   me. I got a really cool shirt for only five dollars, but I'm not
3   sure it was worth my entire family being upset with me.

4   When I really think about the big choices coming up in
5   my life that I have to make, it's a bit overwhelming. Just
6   thinking about things like where to go to college, whether or
7   not to stay with my boyfriend while I'm at college, and even
8   more serious things like my career choice make my mind
9   start spinning!

10   My parents tell me I need to spend more time thinking
11   through my decisions. Just what could the consequences be
12   for each choice? The problem with that idea is that there's
13   no time to sit and think about all the "what ifs." You just
14   kind of have to decide and do it. Maybe that's why I'm
15   sitting here today spending so much time just thinking, so
16   that when the time for a decision arises, all the thinking will
17   already be done, and I'll be able to make a wise choice.

18   They say that with age comes wisdom. Not that I'm
19   wishing to get old, but I sure wish I could skip over all the
20   mistakes I'm going to make along the way!

Discussion Questions

Share some of the decisions you will have to be making in the near future. What or who influences the choices you make? Think of situations when you have made poor choices. What consequences did you suffer because of these? How could you have handled these situations differently? Are there any times when you were torn between making a good or bad choice? What helps you to choose the right thing?

56. Furs Should Be Banished!

1   I have to say that with all the man-made materials
2 available to people today, who in their right mind would still
3 choose to wear a real animal fur? Don't people realize that
4 fur coats and other pieces of fur clothing are a thing of the
5 past?

6   I understand how the whole thing began. I mean, Native
7 Americans and the early settlers had no choice but to kill
8 animals and use their fur for warmth. But ever since the
9 textile mills began, the need for animal furs is non-existent.

10   I recently saw a documentary that showed dogs being
11 skinned alive for their furs. I'd love to force every person
12 wearing a fur coat to sit and watch this film. It's hard to
13 believe these things actually go on, but they do.

14   Some people support the fur industry by saying that
15 mink farms raise minks just for the purpose of providing
16 warm material for coats. They say no animals are taken
17 from the wild, because they are bred right there at the mink
18 farm.

19   Actually, to me that's a lame excuse. The bottom line is
20 the mink farmers are raising animals to kill them for
21 clothing when we have plenty of man-made materials that
22 look just like real fur. Issues always seem to be about
23 making money. Even when you know something you're
24 doing is wrong, if you're making money by doing it, people
25 justify their actions.

26   Even on the anti-fur side, people are taking drastic
27 measures. I read where a woman had orange paint thrown
28 on her as she walked the city streets in her fur coat. She

1 was leaving a theatre performance when an anti-fur
2 protester threw the paint on her. I'm sorry, but that's wrong,
3 too. Can't all of us just sit down together and discuss this
4 problem rationally? I would have one question to ask the
5 pro-fur people: What prestige does it give a person to walk
6 around in a dead animal's fur, anyway?! Personally, I think
7 it's gross. I say buy wool. At least the sheep are still alive!

Discussion Questions

Share your opinion on wearing real fur. Would you ever wear fur? Is it ever right to kill animals? Discuss the idea of using animals to test medicines and observe illnesses.

57. Fear of Flying

1   How is it that fear is able to affect our lives to such a
2 great extent? I'm afraid of heights, of crowds, of waves, and,
3 most of all, flying! I am so tired of being afraid that I even
4 went to a hypnotist. I don't think much was accomplished
5 during the visit, because I still won't climb ladders, go to
6 large parks, swim in the ocean, or fly in an airplane!
7   I'm extremely disappointed in myself for not being able
8 to get over my fear of flying. Members of my Spanish class
9 are in Europe right now, while I'm sitting at home with no
10 friends around. Just because I'm afraid to ride on an
11 airplane, I stayed home. As I sit here alone, I'm wishing I
12 was in Spain. But I also know the reality of my fear, and I
13 realize that I would have panicked in the airport and not
14 gone on the trip, losing several thousand dollars in the
15 process. At least I had the sense to recognize my problem.
16 Now I just have to deal with it.
17   My dad said that if I don't get over this great fear, it
18 could possibly affect my career one day. There was a man
19 newly hired with my dad's company who didn't tell the boss
20 when he interviewed for the job that he was afraid of flying.
21 They hired him and sent him a ticket to go to the corporate
22 office in Chicago for training. Most people would be thrilled
23 about this opportunity, but this man sent the ticket back
24 with a note saying he didn't realize the job required flying,
25 so he regretfully resigned before he even began.
26   A few months later, the man called and said he had
27 gone through intensive counseling for his fear. He wondered
28 if they would consider giving him another chance.

1 Unfortunately for him, the position had long been filled and
2 nothing else was available. This man lost a career with a
3 successful corporation because of his fear of flying.
4   I think we are all afraid of something. That slogan, "no
5 fear," makes me laugh. I don't believe anyone has "no fear."
6 Even my dad, who has fought in two wars, hates snakes!
7 See what I mean? Yet, while I realize it's normal to be afraid
8 of some things, I'm afraid of way too many things. My plan
9 is to reduce my list of fears one by one.
10   I'm going to start small and work my way up to my
11 greatest fears. I thought today I would try climbing up a
12 small ladder in the kitchen. Then tomorrow, I might try an
13 outside ladder. Once I can do that without panicking, I'll be
14 ready to visit an amusement park.
15   You just wait. Talk to me again in a few years and my
16 list will be gone, and I'll be talking to you from Spain. When
17 I get rid of these fears I have, a whole new world awaits me.

Discussion Questions

What are your fears? Think of ways your fears may be
holding you back from fully enjoying your life. How might
you overcome some of your fears? Create your own "fear
reduction" action plan.

58. Don't Let My Mom Die

1   I've heard people say that your life can be turned upside-
2   down in a moment. I guess I never really understood what
3   that meant until this past week. My mom just told me that
4   she has cancer and things don't look very good for her. I
5   think I'm still in shock about it right now, but it's starting
6   to set in to me that she's really sick. She keeps trying to
7   get me to talk to her about it, but I just keep telling her that
8   I won't believe it, that she's going to be fine, and that's the
9   last I want to hear about it.
10   I know that I can't keep pretending that it's not true. I
11   guess I think that if I keep denying the truth about it, it will
12   eventually go away. I just know that I can't go on without
13   my mom. Not yet, anyway. I still have too many years of life
14   to live where I need her. She has to be around for me when
15   I graduate from high school and then from college. And I
16   can't imagine getting married without her being there for me
17   through all the planning. I need her! Can't God see that I will
18   never be OK if he takes her from me so early?
19   Mom and I have always had a very special relationship.
20   During all those times when some of my friends were ready
21   to run away from home because their moms were driving
22   them crazy, I always knew how lucky I was. My mom and I
23   have normal disagreements, but never have I felt that I
24   wanted to have a different mom, or that I ever hated her.
25   She's always been there for me, even when I've messed up
26   really bad.
27   I keep praying that some sort of miracle cure for cancer
28   will happen any day now. She's just too good of a person to

1 make die this way. My dad loves her so much, too. He
2 doesn't deserve to lose the only woman he's ever loved. But
3 most of all, Mom doesn't deserve this. I am so angry right
4 now. How can cancer not care one bit about who it strikes?
5 It almost seems as if the disease looked for the best person
6 in my life to bring down. Maybe that's it, maybe I'm the one
7 who's done something really bad, and God is punishing me
8 for it by taking my mom. Is that it, God? Are you mad at
9 me?
10   I would do anything to take her place right now. You
11 know that, God, don't you?

Discussion Questions

None of us really know when it will be our time to be taken from this earth, but if you knew one of your parents would die soon, how would you want to spend your time together? Would you live in denial, trying to pretend the disease wasn't real until you absolutely had to face it? Explain. Are there certain things you want to do in this life before it's your time to pass on?

59. Does Anyone Know What Love Means?

1   Are there any high school girls or guys who really
2   understand what love is? It seems like everyone says the
3   word a lot, but no one really seems to mean it. I guess I've
4   been brought up in a household where my parents talked to
5   us about love from the time we were little kids. I've always
6   known that I would never tell a guy I loved him unless I was
7   in the relationship for keeps.

8   I have seen so many friends go through broken hearts,
9   and I'm getting pretty tired of hearing about how their
10 boyfriends are so in love with them. Then, you find out that
11 once the guy gets what he wants, he breaks up and is
12 already dating another girl within twenty-four hours! Where
13 is all that love he was telling her about the day before? It's
14 really hard for me to believe that people actually use each
15 other in that way.

16 If I'm dating a guy and he even tries to say the L word
17 to me, I tell him to please stop and really think about what
18 he's about to say. To me, love means commitment. It
19 means that no matter what happens that person is going to
20 be there for me. If we have any problems, we'll work them
21 out together. You don't just break up because you disagree
22 or because you're annoyed by something the other person
23 does. You talk about it. You compromise. You find a way to
24 make it work.

25 I would guess that maybe two percent of teenagers
26 really understand the words "I love you." So, unless you're
27 one of those very few, and you've met another person in that
28 two percent, just save your breath. It's just a heartbreak

1   waiting to happen.

2   You might ask me, "How are you supposed to know if
3 the other person is sincere?" Try dating at least six months
4 before you even think about saying those special words.
5 Then, maybe after a year, if the relationship is still going
6 strong, you might take a chance.

7   As for me, it will probably be after college before I ever
8 believe it when a guy says the L word to me. That's the
9 soonest I think any guy is maybe ready for a serious
10 relationship. Do I sound bitter to you? Yeah, well, maybe
11 that's because I've been one of those girls who gave it all up
12 to someone who said they'd never leave me, and found out
13 they were already texting another girl before we were
14 officially over.

15   Yeah, I'm pretty sure it will be after college before I ever
16 trust another guy. But that's all right. I have lots of things I
17 want to do with my life and lots of goals I plan to achieve.
18 I've got plenty of time to fall in love.

Discussion Questions

What do you think about this girl's opinion on love? Do you feel the L word is used too loosely, without much thought given to the heartache caused when it's spoken too soon? Do girls make the same mistakes as the guys in professing love too soon? Explain. Is it possible to love someone, but realize it's best that you don't stay together? Explain.

60. Do I Have Perseverance?

1   I was reading an article in a recent teen magazine where
2 the author discussed the characteristics of a person who
3 has good values. One character trait he listed captured my
4 attention, because I wasn't really sure if I understood its
5 true meaning. The word was "perseverance." Could you
6 define that?

7   I was so captivated by this word, "perseverance," that I
8 looked up its meaning in the dictionary. If you knew me,
9 you'd know that I don't spend much time looking up words
10 in the dictionary! Well, anyway, according to *The American*
11 *College Dictionary*, perseverance means "steady persistence
12 in a course of action ... continuance in a state of grace to
13 the end."

14   "Wow," I thought to myself. "That's quite a character
15 trait to have." Then, I started thinking about my own
16 personality and asking if I have perseverance. Do I run the
17 race to the finish line? Am I the type of person who doesn't
18 give up when obstacles are in my way? And not only do I not
19 give up, but do I maintain a composed, calm attitude about
20 myself while trying to accomplish a difficult task?

21   After much self-reflection, I have to say I wasn't too
22 disappointed in myself. I am a person who is determined to
23 achieve my goals. I like to finish what I start, and I do keep
24 trying when something gets in my way. In fact, at times
25 obstacles can make me even more determined to get where
26 I want to be.

27   But, there is one part of perseverance I sincerely need to
28 work on. It's that "state of grace" part. Why does that have

1 to be mentioned in the definition, which I, of course, believe
2 in? If I'm honest with myself, I have to admit that I have a
3 long way to go on having grace when I hit failure.
4   How are you supposed to stay all happy and smiley-
5 faced when, for example, I'm trying to get into an eastern
6 school and the rejection letters start to arrive? OK, I do
7 keep sending out applications, and I'm not giving up, but
8 there are a lot of tears cried after each letter is read. Isn't
9 that normal? How is anyone ever able to truly achieve the
10 trait of perseverance in their life if you're supposed to accept
11 obstacles with grace?
12   I've been thinking, though. Maybe tears are acceptable.
13 I mean, we are all human, it's not like I rant and rave and
14 have a temper tantrum. Perhaps a good cry when running
15 smack into an obstacle on life's path is nature's survival
16 tactic. Crying releases stress. And when all the tears have
17 been shed, I find myself with renewed energy to, once again,
18 tackle the goal at hand.
19   I'd like to say I have perseverance. I guess I'm just still
20 trying to figure out what perseverance is all about. I want to
21 be a person considered honorable, so I'll keep trying. Hey,
22 that's what perseverance is really all about! I'll just try
23 shedding a few less tears from now on when things don't
24 work out my way! But, I will never give up on reaching my
25 goals.

Discussion Questions

Do you feel you are a person who perseveres? What obstacles might cause you to give up on a dream goal for yourself? What do you feel is meant when it is said we should be "gracious" in defeat? How do you handle defeat? Think of examples of times you have persevered despite obstacles in your way.

61. Divorce Blues

1   I'm sitting in my living room watching my mom as she
2 pushes the lawn mower around and around our yard. It's
3 about ninety degrees outside, and she looks pretty
4 exhausted. I guess she has about half of the yard done.
5 Meanwhile, I'm thinking I'll just help myself to another
6 glass of iced tea, then turn on my favorite soap opera.

7   Sounds rude, doesn't it? Well, you know, there was a
8 time I would have been the first person out there offering to
9 help my mom cut the grass. I would do anything for my
10 mom. But she just told me yesterday that she's serving
11 Dad divorce papers. Out of the blue, just like that, she's
12 divorcing my dad! I am so mad at her that I'm not sure if I
13 ever plan to talk to her again. It's been pretty easy for me
14 to avoid her for the past thirty-six hours. I guess the next
15 thirty-six years shouldn't be much harder!

16   I know I sound terrible, but I'm really a very loving child.
17 I've always been the one of us four kids who does what I'm
18 told, when I'm told, and without any attitude. I don't know,
19 maybe I'm tired of playing this role. Mom seems to have
20 decided she's tired of playing wife. If she's allowed to switch
21 gears on all of us, why can't I?

22   Maybe if I understood why this is happening, I could
23 accept the divorce easier. When I tried talking to Mom about
24 it, all she would say is it has nothing to do with us kids, that
25 the problems are between her and Dad. Oh yeah, she added
26 some stupid line about "growing apart" or something like
27 that. What does *that* mean? *Growing apart?*

28   Doesn't she know that when two people "grow apart"

1 you have to work to get things back together? Geez, I feel
2 like I know more about marriage than she does. She told me
3 she doesn't want us kids to turn against her or Dad, so she
4 feels the less we know about the details of the divorce the
5 better it will be.
6   But I think that's nonsense! We're not little kids
7 anymore! My sisters and brother are in their early twenties
8 and I'm eighteen! I mean, all four of us are old enough to be
9 married ourselves, by law, anyway. So, come on, Mom, help
10 us understand what is going on!
11   *(Pause, thinking and watching out the window)* Every time
12 I think I want Mom to tell me the real reason she's divorcing
13 Dad, I start to get scared, because what if she tells me he
14 has a girlfriend or something like that? Then, I would hate
15 him. And I don't want to hate either of my parents. We really
16 need to talk about this, though, don't you think?
17   *(Look out the window again.)* I'm not going to cut the
18 grass for Mom, but maybe, just this once, I'll bring her out
19 a glass of iced tea.

Discussion Questions

Just how much information do you feel the children of
divorcing parents should be told? Do you feel it's possible for
people who have "grown apart" to get back together? How
is it possible for people to stay connected whenever we all
change as we grow older? Should children stay neutral in a
divorce, as long as both parents treat them well and make
it known that they are loved by both?

62. Depressed Dad

1   Lately, my dad has been acting so strange. We've always
2   had a great relationship. Anytime I needed someone to talk
3   to, I knew I could go to my dad. He's always loved me
4   unconditionally and has never passed judgment. In fact, all
5   of my friends say they wish he was their dad.

6   But just recently, Dad has been acting different. He
7   spends a lot of time sleeping, and he never wants to do
8   anything anymore. He used to be the one who had endless
9   energy. Even if he'd worked twelve hours that day, Dad
10   came to my ball games at night. Just this week he missed
11   both of my softball games.

12   My mom passed away five years ago. So, it's not like I
13   can really use that as an excuse for his behavior. By now,
14   everyone in the family seems used to her not being here
15   anymore. Of course, there are times I still miss her terribly.
16   But, we've all had to adjust to what life is now and keep
17   living. Until now, I thought things were going pretty well.

18   Dad hasn't been eating enough, and I can see he's lost
19   weight. I usually do the cooking, and if I must say so, I do
20   a pretty good job. Unfortunately, I burned the burgers last
21   night. Dad was really upset with me over it and told me I try
22   to do too many things at one time, and that I need to be
23   more careful. Two months ago, he would have teased me
24   about the whole incident, and then he would have said,
25   "Don't worry, grab your coat and let's eat out!"

26   Instead, he stomped off to his bedroom and went to
27   sleep until morning. The longer this goes on, the more I
28   wonder if Dad is depressed. Is that possible? I really don't

1 know who to talk to about this.
2   I just want my old dad back.

Discussion Questions

What are the signs of depression? Does the father in this monologue show any signs of depression? What resources are available to anyone in this girl's position? (The teacher should have local resources available to share with the group. Discuss these resources with the students.)

63. Dating Just to Be Dating

1   Recently, I discovered something about myself that I
2 don't particularly like very much. When I look back at the
3 last few guys I've dated, I noticed that I've really lowered my
4 standards! I have to ask myself, "What were you thinking?"
5   At first, I thought the guys were the problem. I mean,
6 none of the last three guys even had a job. They were
7 always looking for money from either their parents, or me! I
8 found myself many a Friday and Saturday night watching
9 videos we rented with newspaper coupons — *Special, Two*
10 *for the Price of One!* When that became the exciting date
11 night for my most recent boyfriend, I knew the relationship
12 was in big time trouble. When he started asking what my
13 mom was cooking for supper so that we could eat in with
14 the parents, that was the final red flag. It was over.
15   Lately, though, I decided that to be fair I have to accept
16 part of the blame for these bad relationships. After all, I did
17 agree to date these guys. I must have been desperate! Well,
18 desperation is no longer a word in my vocabulary. You got
19 that, friends? No more dating losers, just so I have a guy to
20 be with on the weekends.
21   In fact, this Friday night, I'm planning on going shopping
22 at the mall with my mom. Ten months ago, that would shout
23 *desperation!* louder than any other plan. But now, a night
24 out with my mom sounds so much more inviting than
25 spending my time with one more deadbeat guy looking for a
26 free place to hang out.
27   I can name five things I'd rather do than hang out with
28 one more loser:

1   One: I could give my dog a bath. Don't laugh. My dog is
2 nicer than most guys.
3   Two: I could wash my hair. Hey, I love my hair. I need
4 to start treating it with more compassion and care.
5   Three: I could start a Girls Club, and we could meet on
6 the weekends. Definitely, no guys allowed.
7   Four: I could read a romantic novel and keep reminding
8 myself that there might actually be a guy like the main
9 character out there waiting for me.
10   Five: I could start exercising. There's nothing like a good
11 workout to ease the stress of not having a guy.
12   All right, I can do this. I have a plan. *(Pause)* Just
13 promise me one thing — whenever you meet an available Mr.
14 Right who has a job, can buy his own supper, and owns a
15 car, please give him my number.

Discussion Questions

What qualities do you look for in a guy you want to date? Share what behaviors are "red flags" to you when you're dating a guy. Do you ever find yourself dating someone just to pass the time, until the right guy comes along? Are there any activities you could add to this girl's list of things to do instead of hanging out with a loser?

64. Custody Issues

1   I can't believe I am in the middle of a custody battle. I
2 am in high school — the last thing I should be mixed up in
3 is having to decide whether to live with my mom or my dad.
4 Things were easy when I was younger; my parents had to
5 abide by what the judge declared. But, now that I'm of age,
6 everyone has decided that I should make a choice and stop
7 all of this back and forth drama that has gone on for the
8 past eight years.
9   I guess I'm somewhat at fault for this new battle. After
10 eight years of packing up my things every two weeks, taking
11 turns spending time at Mom's, then Dad's, it just finally got
12 to me. When I forgot my blow dryer at my mom's and Dad
13 didn't have one, I blew up! I'm so tired of trying to please
14 my parents when they're the ones who don't know how to
15 get along.
16   Sure, I know what you're thinking, "Why don't you just
17 buy two of everything so that you don't have to keep
18 dragging things back and forth to your parents' houses?"
19 Sounds like an easy solution, unless you're the one who has
20 to buy two of everything. My parents say they don't have the
21 money to do that, and it's unnecessary to spend money like
22 that, when I can just be responsible and pack my things up
23 each time I visit the other parent.
24   Unfortunately, my parents don't seem to understand the
25 stress I am living under right now. I'm getting ready for
26 college exams, I'm on the basketball team, and I'm an
27 officer in Student Council and National Honor Society. How
28 am I supposed to never forget anything? I keep trying to

1 make them both proud of me, and sometimes I think it's
2 working. But most of the time, I feel as if I'm a little pawn
3 in their game to make each other more miserable than they
4 already are.
5   This past nine weeks my grades went down somewhat,
6 that's why Mom and Dad have decided that I need to pick a
7 place and stay put. While that truly sounds inviting, I will
8 hurt one of them terribly if I don't choose them. How could
9 they put me in this position?
10   I wonder what both of them would say if I suddenly
11 asked to go live with Grandma? That might solve this
12 problem for all of us. Hmmmm, sounds like a plan.

Discussion Question

How can parents make life easier for their children when there is a divorce situation? Would any of you be willing to share what works for your family, if your parents are divorced? What might be a solution for the girl speaking in this monologue? At what age do you feel a child should have a say in their own custody agreement?

65. Cosmetic Surgery

1   A few years ago it seemed that it was only on television
2 we saw all of these beautiful girls with perfect bodies. You
3 know what I mean, the thirty-six, twenty-four, thirty-six
4 type. I suppose in glamour magazines the same mold could
5 be found. But at least, we as a group of young girls, could
6 look at these images and rationalize by saying to each
7 other, "Aw, you know we could look like that if we were in
8 Hollywood. All you need is money and a good plastic
9 surgeon. And half of these pictures in the magazines, well,
10 computer graphics take care of all those girls' flaws."
11   But man, when I look around today, it's not just the
12 girls in the movies and magazines that are looking perfect.
13 It's girls I go to school with every day! I don't know where
14 they're getting the money from, but they leave school in
15 June a thirty-four A and come back in the fall with thirty-six
16 Ds. Don't start laughing now, because you know it's true.
17   Personally, I never really worried about what size chest I
18 had. I actually prefer to be smaller. Those big chests just
19 seem to get in the way when you like to play sports, which
20 I do. But, the more I see how common and accepted
21 cosmetic surgery is becoming, the more I think I would like
22 to have a nose job. *(The actor can change this body part to
23 fit their own feelings of inadequacy.)* I mean, I have not liked
24 my nose since fourth grade, when it seemed to grow to a
25 size my body just never caught up to!
26   I guess it's really a personal matter. Sometimes I think
27 that if changing something about yourself makes you feel
28 better and gives you greater self-esteem, then go for it.

1 Other times, it just seems like an exaggerated amount of
2 vanity and a huge waste of money. Think about it — with the
3 money I would spend on a nose job, I could do a lot of good
4 for my community. I could buy food for the shelter in town,
5 or I could donate it to a poor single mom who's just barely
6 getting by.
7   Then I think of all the social events at school I stay home
8 from because I feel less pretty than the other girls. I know
9 it's stupid. Everyone has something they're hung up about,
10 but my nose truly bothers me. My mom and dad support
11 this idea wholeheartedly. I guess they've seen how this has
12 affected me over the years. In fact, my mom encourages me
13 to go ahead with the idea. Don't get me wrong, she doesn't
14 push me, she loves me just the way I am. But, she thinks
15 I'll be happier with myself, and therefore, life in general.
16   Do you know anybody who's gone through this? I'd love
17 to hear what the outcomes of their choices were. I'll keep
18 you posted on what I decide.

Discussion Questions

What is your opinion on people altering their looks to feel better about themselves? Is there anything about yourself for which you would have cosmetic surgery? Do you feel Hollywood and the whole movie industry influences a women's negative feeling about herself? Explain.

66. Computers – Does the Good Outweigh the Bad?

1   We're having this huge debate right now at my house
2   over whether or not we need to keep our computer. Can you
3   even believe my parents would consider getting rid of the
4   computer? I mean, how does a person exist in the twenty-
5   first century without one! You may as well cut yourself off
6   from civilization! I'm guessing that if they get rid of the
7   computer, the next thing to go will be my cell phone, and
8   who knows what will go after that. I'm thinking my parents
9   are entering some "return to the days of old" zone where life
10 was less technical.
11   But let's face it, I wouldn't be able to finish half of my
12 homework if we weren't online. Most research reports
13 require at least one online source. How would I ever
14 translate my Spanish homework if I couldn't use the online
15 translation dictionary to check my work? I could go on and
16 on about the ways the computer helps me in school. But
17 every time I plead my case to Dad, he has an answer.
18 *(Imitate father's voice)* "You can go to the library and use the
19 computer there." Or, "You shouldn't be letting the computer
20 do your translating homework, anyway." Or better yet, "I
21 think my old set of encyclopedias are still at Grandma and
22 Grandpa's. Maybe I'll go get those for you this weekend."
23   I try to explain to Dad that I can't get into the library at
24 ten o'clock at night, which is when I'm getting my
25 homework done half the time. By the time I get home from
26 practice, it gets pretty late. And, I truly do my own
27 translating. I just like to be able to make sure it's right after
28 I do it myself. Honest! When Dad mentioned his old

1 encyclopedias, I *think* he was joking. He's an intelligent
2 man; he obviously must understand that the encyclopedias
3 he used are practically historical archives by now. News
4 changes by the minute.
5   I guess there is one little part of this debate I'm leaving
6 out. The whole thing that got my mom and dad going about
7 this is the fact that I'm a computer addict. I admit it. But
8 what teenager isn't? My parents say we spend no "quality
9 time" together anymore, that all I do is sit at the computer.
10 That's not entirely true, though. I do play sports at school.
11 But once I get home, I guess I spend a lot of time on the
12 computer.
13   Most of the time, I'm doing my homework. It's just that
14 while I'm working, my friends and I IM each other and talk
15 about what's going on with everyone. The difference between
16 my parents and me is that they grew up doing one thing at
17 a time. I'm perfectly capable of doing my homework while
18 I'm talking to my friends online. Everyone does it. I'm even
19 on the honor roll every nine weeks.
20   I guess I'm wondering what all of you do at your house.
21 I'm willing to compromise here, but to totally take my
22 computer away ... well, that just stinks.

Discussion Questions

What are the ground rules of computer use at your
house? Do you feel technology interferes with personal, one-
on-one communication among family and friends? How
helpful is the computer with your schoolwork? Could you
succeed without a computer in your home?

67. Can We Go Back to Being Friends?

1   I find myself in an awful position right now. I can see
2 that I broke a cardinal rule of dating: Never date your best
3 friend. I've heard people warn against this, but when my guy
4 best friend and I started thinking maybe there was more to
5 the friendship than just friends, we both decided to try
6 moving on to the next level.

7   Big mistake. The problem is I don't think he is feeling
8 the same way. He seems perfectly happy in a relationship
9 with me. But I'm feeling trapped. I just want to be able to
10 do something without him once in awhile.

11   When we were just friends, we did do everything
12 together. But now that you add in all the hugging and
13 kissing he wants to do, I just want to yell, "Leave me alone!
14 Just let me run through the fields, free of anyone touching
15 me and wanting to make out." Maybe I'm just not ready for
16 an intense relationship yet.

17   I feel really bad. Josh and I seem to understand each
18 other and are into the same things. We were friends for so
19 long before we dated that I thought this was going to be the
20 guy I married. I've always heard that it's best to be friends
21 first, because friendship is what always lasts in a
22 relationship, no matter how old you get. No one warned me
23 of how I would feel if I decided I didn't want Josh as my
24 boyfriend.

25   Maybe we just need some space. I need time to just
26 hang out with friends. When I'm with Josh, I feel the
27 pressure of being more than that all the time. I've tried
28 explaining this to him, but he doesn't seem to understand.

1 He says he's so in love with me that he doesn't want to
2 spend time with other people.
3   I don't know if we can go backwards in our relationship,
4 but I'd like to try. Are girls and guys able to be just friends
5 after they've taken the plunge into something more? All I
6 know is Josh and I can't keep on this way. I'm being
7 smothered. We either need to go back to friendship or our
8 entire relationship needs to end.
9   Take my advice, girls. If you've got a terrific friendship
10 going on with a guy, just leave it where it is. You'll be much
11 happier.

Discussion Questions

Has it ever worked for you to take a boy and girl friend
relationship back to a level of just friends after dating? If so,
how were you both able to make that work? Is it possible for
girl and guy best friends to be "just friends" and never
venture into something more, or is more inevitable?

68. Can I Take Care of My Baby?

1   I'm sitting here in my hospital bed, wondering what step
2   in my life to take next. I just had a baby, a beautiful baby
3   girl. She's absolutely perfect, ten tiny little fingers and ten
4   adorable toes. She's just waiting for someone to love her
5   and teach her everything she needs to know about the
6   world.

7   My heart is filled with such joy, but, at the same time,
8   it also feels as if someone has taken and torn it into pieces.
9   All of my family and friends keep encouraging me to sign
10   adoption papers. Up until the birth of my little girl I was
11   leaning toward going along with an adoption. But now, I
12   can't explain the way I feel. This tiny being is a part of me.
13   She's a real, alive-and-kicking baby! And I gave her life! Me!
14   I've never done anything important, ever — until now!

15   Since I haven't signed any adoption papers yet, I've
16   been able to take care of Abby while we're still in the
17   hospital. That's what I'm calling her, Abigail Lea. Isn't her
18   name beautiful? Abby and I are already bonded. She grabs
19   my finger in her tiny hand and holds on for dear life. I feel
20   as if she's already communicating to me that she wants to
21   stay with me.

22   Mom and Dad, of course, are the "reality experts." They
23   keep saying that Abby will have a better life if I give her to
24   a childless couple. They remind me that I am only
25   seventeen, and that if I give Abby up, I can go to college and
26   start my life anew. Don't they know that for the past nine
27   months I've already thought of that scenario versus me
28   keeping Abby! Every waking moment I've struggled with the

1   idea of which path to take. All I know is that I can't choose
2   to keep Abby unless my parents agree. I would need their
3   help and financial support. Don't even ask where Abby's
4   father is, he's off enjoying his freshman year of college,
5   pretending as if we don't exist.
6   If I can just get Mom to hold Abby, I know she would go
7   along with me keeping her. Right now, she and Dad have an
8   agreement to not see Abby. They're afraid to get attached,
9   and then be swayed to let me keep her. They feel the
10 adoption is best, so they don't want any influences to make
11 them change their minds.
12   Man, my mind is racing and won't stop. I know Abby
13 would have a wonderful life with some couple who's praying
14 night and day for their own baby. But she'd have a wonderful
15 life with me, too! My parents are good people, and I know I'd
16 be the best mother I could be for her. I just don't know what
17 to do.

Discussion Questions

Under what circumstances do you feel a teenage, unwed mother should keep her baby? What options might this young girl have other than adoption or raising the baby herself? Is it fair for her to expect her parents to help her support the baby? Place yourself in this situation. How might you feel about having a baby to raise?

69. Body Image

1   My friends and I had taken a survey recently about how
2 girls feel about their bodies. Everyone seems to have
3 something they're hung up about. Take me, for instance, I
4 have real issues about my skin. I mean, I've been breaking
5 out since I was thirteen. It doesn't seem to matter how
6 many different medicines I try, or doctors I see. I'm learning
7 to deal with it.

8   Right now, my best friend is working a summer job,
9 saving her money so she can have rhinoplasty. Do you know
10 what that is? Don't worry about it, I didn't either until my
11 friend explained it to me. It means she's going to have a
12 nose job. Honestly, I say good for her! If it will make her feel
13 better about herself to fix her nose, which, by the way, is a
14 little big, then go for it! Actually, I think she's beautiful just
15 the way she is, but she doesn't see herself that way.

16   One thing I wasn't surprised to hear were so many girls
17 complaining about their weight. Our country puts so much
18 stress on being thin, that it's really unfair to people who are
19 naturally larger framed. And the weird thing I've noticed
20 about weight issues is that every twenty years or so, the
21 "in" shape changes! Look at the old pictures of Marilyn
22 Monroe. Nowadays she'd be called fat! These Hollywood
23 actresses who think it's trendy to look anorexic are crazy!
24 But that seems to be the trend teenage girls are copying
25 right now.

26   Body image is something our generation needs to focus
27 on helping each other through. Everyone has issues. But we
28 girls need to stick together and encourage each other to

1   love ourselves. I'm not saying it's OK to gorge yourself and
2   not worry about your weight, or to have hyper kinky hair and
3   not try to tame it down a bit. I'm saying that what's
4   important is learning to love ourselves for who we are and
5   how we were made.
6   If we all just do the best we can with what we've got and
7   learn to be content with that, we could spend our time
8   focusing on something more interesting than ourselves!

Discussion Questions

If you could choose one thing about yourself you would change, what would it be and why? How can we help each other to be accepting of ourselves and others? Share some of your qualities with which you are satisfied. Are you able to share some positive comments with the others in this group about yourselves?

70. Black, White, and Gray

1   Maybe you can help me understand the difference
2 between times it's OK to "cheat" and times it's not. I mean,
3 I know it's not right to purposely give a person back the
4 wrong amount of change, hoping they don't notice, just so
5 you can pocket the difference. But there are times when it
6 seems OK to save yourself a few bucks.

7   Take last week. I went to the movies with my friend and
8 both of us are really short, so depending on what we wear,
9 we can pass for the children's ticket. It is three dollars less
10 than an adult's, so you can understand why we would want
11 to do this. I mean, the food is so expensive there. They don't
12 think twice about charging us three times what a bag of
13 popcorn should cost. So, why not save myself a few dollars
14 getting in? I end up spending it on food anyway. In the long
15 run, they still get their money.

16   Oh, and another place that charges way too much to get
17 in is the county fair. Personally, I don't think you should
18 have to pay anything to get into a fair. All you do once you
19 get inside is spend money on rides, food, and games. So,
20 why do they charge you to get in? Well, my friend and I have
21 this one figured out, too. Either we crawl under a back fence
22 we find down by the horse stalls, or we call a friend who's
23 already inside to ask what the hand stamp of the day is.
24 Then we just mark our own hands. We've never been
25 stopped once.

26   What about when you go out to dinner with your
27 parents? I mean, the only way my family can afford to go to
28 a nice restaurant is if my sister and I say that we're still on

1 the children's menu. I guess a few waitresses have raised
2 their eyebrows in doubt, but they still give us the children's
3 prices, no questions asked. So, why not?
4   I know we're not really doing the right thing, but can you
5 understand my justification of what we do? And just tell
6 me, who in this world *never* does something a little bit
7 wrong? I mean, nobody's perfect, right?

Discussion Questions

Share your opinions about each of the situations this speaker talks about: the movies, the fair, a restaurant. Is it really OK to pretend to be a different age just to save money? Would your conscience allow you to do this? Can you think of a time when you "cheated" in some way? How is cheating a business out of income any different from stealing?

7 1. Bench Warmer Blues

1 Do you ever feel as if you're never quite good enough? I
2 have been feeling that way for the past six years. No matter
3 how hard I work, or how much I practice, I am never more
4 than the bench warmer for our school teams.
5   I love to play basketball and softball. My dad has helped
6 me learn the games since I was six. When I was finally old
7 enough to try out for a team, I was thrilled. And that first
8 year I kept the bench warm really didn't bother me. But the
9 longer you sit there, year after year, it gets really old. I think
10 there are permanent groove marks on the backside of my
11 pants from sitting on the bench so long!
12   My parents are very supportive. They come to every
13 game, just in case I might happen to get in. I can count on
14 one hand how many times I've actually got to play in a real
15 game. Dad keeps reminding me that everyone on the team
16 has a role they play. My role is to be the practice player that
17 the starters play against. I understand that's an important
18 part to play, because the starters need people willing to
19 scrimmage against them in practice. You would think that
20 just once, though, I might get to experience the feeling of
21 being a part of the actual game.
22   Here it is, my senior year approaching, and I finally
23 thought I'd be on the starting lineup of both my basketball
24 and softball teams. Wrong. A girl from another state moved
25 in and took my spot! That's when I decided I'd finally had
26 enough. I told my parents I wanted to either move out to the
27 county schools where I know I'd be starting, since the
28 competition is not as tough, or I want to quit.

1   Both Dad and Mom said we cannot move out of our
2   house just so I can play high school softball and basketball.
3   They don't want me to quit, either, after I've stuck it out for
4   so many years. I even tried to see if they'd pay tuition for me
5   to go to one of the outlying schools, but no, they say,
6   "Disappointment is a part of life. You need to keep your chin
7   up and keep trying." But they have to understand, don't
8   they, that enough is enough! I am so embarrassed and
9   humiliated.

10   When the coach heard I might quit, she came and gave
11   me a pep talk about how important I am to the team, and
12   that she wants me to realize how much I help the team by
13   always being there. She said that this year I'm number six
14   off the bench, so even if I don't start, I'll probably play every
15   game. I know she's not the type to come and beg more than
16   once, so if I say, "I quit," that decision will be final.

17   Honestly, I don't want to quit, but could she put that
18   promise of playing every game in writing? I think that then,
19   and only then, I'll stay on the team.

Discussion Questions

Do you feel the coach is right to play a new student in front of a senior, who has been on the team every year of high school? Would you be willing to be a "bench warmer" year after year? If you already are, how do you feel about that? Do you think this girl should quit? Would you?

72. Becoming Who We Are

1   Do you ever have days when you wish that just this once
2   everything would go your way? No matter how hard I try to
3   do everything right, somehow something gets messed up.
4   The weird thing is, I'm just now starting to realize how every
5   piece to the puzzle called "my life" fits together in the end.
6   The day finally arrives when you look at certain events and
7   you say, "Wow, if that bad thing hadn't happened, this good
8   thing wouldn't have happened either!"
9   When you're going through a really tough time, it's hard
10 to accept the fact that there's a plan for everything. I mean,
11 when my mom died from alcoholism three years ago, I
12 wasn't sure if I could go on for one more day. At first, I lived
13 one hour at a time. Gradually, I was able to progress to one
14 day at a time. Life is still really difficult without my mom
15 here, but I'm finally able to go on with my life, not thinking
16 about her death every minute.
17 Because of Mom's experience, I wanted to learn all I
18 could about alcoholism. I'm now helping other children of
19 alcoholics cope with this huge problem through AA. The
20 organization has a chapter just for the family members,
21 helping them learn how to live with an alcoholic.
22 Today, a young girl confided to me that she had
23 considered suicide, but after she and I talked, she changed
24 her mind. She told me that I had given her hope. What an
25 awesome feeling that was to hear someone tell me that I
26 helped them choose to live. That makes me realize that my
27 mom's death helped bring me to this point. It helps me
28 understand that Mom's death was not as meaningless as I

1   thought. In some roundabout way, Mom helped another
2   person stay alive, too. Maybe that sounds silly to you, but to
3   me, it makes me feel proud.
4   I was having trouble finding pride for my mother. This
5   whole incident makes me understand that even bad things,
6   horrible things, can have a purpose for good. We just have
7   to be willing to hear the message being sent.
8   *(Looking heavenward)* Thanks, Mom, for helping me to
9   find a purpose for my life. Your weaknesses have helped me
10 to find my strength. There's nothing better a mother can do
11 for her child.

Discussion Questions

Think about a very positive experience you've had in your life. Now think back on all the different events which led up to this event. Share this with our group. Are you able to think of any sad event, which made no sense at the time, but now you are able to see how it fit into the scheme of your life to create good?

73. Baby Blues

1   All right, I know I'm going to sound selfish, but I can't
2 help it. My new baby sister is driving me crazy! All she does
3 for the entire day is sleep, cry, and dirty her diaper. I haven't
4 had a good night's sleep since she came home from the
5 hospital three weeks ago. If my mom and dad thought I was
6 mad when they told me they were *having* her, you can
7 imagine how mad I am now that she's *here!*
8   My friends try to encourage me by saying how fortunate
9 I am to have a baby sister. I say, "I'm seventeen-years-old!
10 What do I need with a baby sister now?" Sure, when I was
11 growing up it might have been nice to have someone to play
12 with, but now? What are we supposed to have in common
13 besides the same genetic parents?
14   My mom is already asking me to baby-sit so she can go
15 out to the grocery store or the post office. I feel like saying,
16 "Wait a minute. Who is it that chose to have this baby? Not
17 me! Why do I have to baby-sit?"
18   I know that I sound pathetic. Like I said before, I can't
19 help it. It seems like the entire household is changed
20 because of her, and quite frankly, I liked things the way they
21 were. I used to be able to sleep in on Saturday mornings.
22 Now my mom wakes me up by nine, just so I can give her
23 some help around the house.
24   Yesterday, that baby threw up formula all down my back.
25 I was furious! First of all, why should I be the one feeding
26 her, and secondly, I don't want a baby! I'm only seventeen!
27 *(Pause, thinking a moment)* I will admit, she is really
28 precious when she's sleeping. And sometimes, she does

1   this cute thing with her hand. She actually grabs hold of my
2   finger and won't let go. It's like she's saying, "Hey, Sis, let
3   me hold onto you. I need you." That is definitely an
4   awesome moment when she does that.
5   *(Sigh)* Do you know that I think she's starting to know
6   the difference between Mom and me? She must be really
7   smart. Well, of course she is, she's my sister! Wow, I'm
8   starting to make it sound like she's not so bad sometimes.
9   I'm surprising myself with the things I'm saying. Could it
10 possibly be that I'm actually getting used to her?
11   No, I'm definitely not used to her yet, but ... *maybe* I'm
12 starting to like her.

Discussion Questions

Share how you feel about your siblings. Are you friends, as well as siblings? Tell some of the pros and cons of having brothers and sisters. How would you feel about having a new baby in the house when you're seventeen? If you are an only child, do you like it that way, or do you wish for a brother or a sister?

74. Appreciating Education

1   When I sit and listen to students talking to each other,
2 lots of times they're complaining about school. I'm guilty of
3 it myself. And why is that? My school is clean, and for the
4 most part, a very safe place to be. Do we dislike coming
5 here just because we're told we have to come? I mean, if
6 you look around school, it's not such a bad place to be.

7   Our school's principal recently traveled to an island off
8 the coast of Australia. He told us how he had to go by foot
9 up the side of a mountain, walk across a rope bridge that
10 hung over a steep ravine, then walk another mile or so to
11 get to the local school. The children have no books. In order
12 to write down their thoughts, they have to use a pointed
13 stick and scrape their letters in the dirt. There is no school
14 house. The children meet under a tree for class. After their
15 day in school, these kids have hours of work to complete for
16 their family. Many of them have to hunt for food, and if they
17 have no success, they just don't eat that day. But, they
18 never miss school.

19   Their parents know the value an education will give their
20 children. It's their hope that one day their child can help
21 their community live life more fully because of the
22 knowledge they've gained through their studies.

23   Then our principal challenged all of us to look around.
24 He wanted us to notice what a nice place our school is and
25 just how many opportunities we take for granted. When we
26 complain about the school's food, maybe we should realize
27 how many students in the world go to school hungry. When
28 we are upset because we have homework, perhaps we

1   should be thankful to have a home with electricity that lights
2   up a room for us so that we can do our homework. And
3   when kids think it's funny to break pencils in half just for
4   the heck of it, maybe we should remember the students on
5   that island who would consider even a broken half of a pencil
6   a treasure.
7   I know that when my principal was finished speaking to
8   us we all started seeing our school through different eyes.
9   The walls seem a little bit brighter and the books a little bit
10 newer. Even the teachers don't seem so bad anymore. He
11 made me realize that I need to appreciate the education I'm
12 getting and make the most of it. I try to have a good attitude
13 each day and be a good role model for other teens. And
14 when I think of those students on the island carefully
15 crossing that steep ravine on a rope bridge every day, even
16 my long bus rides don't seem so bad anymore.

Discussion Questions

Would you be able to handle living in a remote area such as the one described in this monologue? Explain. Are there things you complain about that you now believe aren't quite so bad? What complaints do you have with your school that you believe are valid and not just griping comments? What are the things you appreciate and enjoy most about your school?

75. Am I Able to Forgive?

1   My mom always says that to be a loving family member
2 and a true friend, you need to understand how forgiveness
3 fits into your relationships. I never really thought much
4 about forgiveness, especially not in my friendships, because
5 everything's always been cool between my friends and me.
6 But right now, unless I can find it in my heart to forgive one
7 of my friends, I'd say our friendship is over.
8   You see, last week I confided in Jen that I had cheated
9 on a test. I truly never do that, but the night before the test
10 I didn't feel well at all, so I didn't get the chance to study
11 much. I know it was a stupid thing to do, but I got really
12 confused on one part and the kid next to me moved his arm
13 so I could see his paper.
14   Like I said, I know I shouldn't have looked, but I did. I
15 felt guilty about the whole thing afterward, that's probably
16 why I told my best friend about it. I thought she'd just listen
17 and let me vent and then forget about it. But oh no, when
18 we got our papers back and Jen failed the test, but I
19 passed, she went to the teacher after class and told on me!
20 I got in all kinds of trouble at school and at home. I still
21 can't believe she did that!
22   Jen tried apologizing to me last night. My mom made
23 me talk to her. Jen said that she realizes now she should
24 never have told on me, that I was the one who did
25 something wrong, and if I wanted to live with the guilt, that
26 should have been my decision. She claims that she was
27 just so mad that she failed the test and I passed by
28 cheating that without taking any time to think about it, she

1 told. As soon as she did, she says that she wanted to take
2 the words back.
3   I never said a word while she talked on and on. When it
4 was finally silent, I asked, "Are you finished?" When she
5 answered yes, I said, "Good-bye," and hung up the phone. I
6 am just not ready to talk to her yet.
7   Mom says that I really need to think about this. She said
8 that I know what I did was wrong, and Jen has apologized
9 for betraying me. She also suggested I think about all the
10 good things my friendship with Jen has brought to me and
11 decide if all the years of friendship are worth throwing away
12 over this one painful incident. I could maybe even find it in
13 my heart to forgive Jen, and start our friendship over.
14   I don't know. Right now, I'm still too hurt to decide.

Discussion Questions

Have you ever betrayed a friendship, or had a friend betray you? What would you do in this situation? Share suggestions on how to forgive those who hurt you. Define your definition of "true friendship."